# COGNITIVE-PERCEPTUAL-MOTOR DYSFUNCTION

# COGNITIVE PERCEPTUAL MOTOR DYSFUNCTION

*from research to practice*

eli z. rubin
jean s. braun
gayle r. beck
lela a. llorens

*Wayne State University Press*
*Detroit 1972*

Published simultaneously in Canada
by the Copp Clark Publishing Company
517 Wellington Street, West
Toronto 2B, Canada.

Lafayette Clinic Monographs in Psychiatry, number 5

Library of Congress Cataloging In Publication Data
Main entry under title:

Cognitive-perceptual-motor dysfunction.

  (Lafayette Clinic monographs in psychiatry, no. 5)
Bibliography: pp. 164–67.
  1. Child psychiatry. 2. Slow learning children.
I. Rubin, Eli Z. II. Series: Lafayette Clinic,
Detroit. Monographs in psychiatry, no. 5.
RJ499.C59       618.92' 8' 9       77-157415

ISBN 0-8143-1451-1

# Lafayette Clinic Monographs in Psychiatry

The Lafayette Clinic is a 145-bed psychiatric research and teaching unit of the Department of Mental Health, State of Michigan, and of Wayne State University. From the clinic's inception in 1955, research in many aspects of mental and emotional illnesses has been a major responsibility. The research programs have been interdisciplinary in nature, and have brought to bear the insights, methods, and theoretical conceptions of anthropology, biochemistry, pharmacology, physiology, psychiatry, psychology, and sociology upon the complex problems that characterize these disturbances to which modern man is heir.

The Lafayette Clinic Monographs in Psychiatry have been designed to present the results of certain basic research and clinical investigations completed at the Lafayette Clinic. Because of the length and content of such studies, their publication in monograph form is more appropriate than the usual method of reporting in scientific journals. It is hoped that these multiple efforts will help in the further evolution of a significant foundation for understanding, control, and reduction of mental and emotional illnesses.

# contents

Contents

# tables

# figures

# preface

This work is based on the premise that the population of emotionally disturbed children is made up of many subgroups and that it is important to differentiate among these groups if appropriate treatment is to be given. We are not referring to traditional diagnostic categories employed in a psychiatric clinic but to the principle that children may arrive at a state of maladjustment through many avenues, not the least of which is that a child himself may be constitutionally constructed in a way that makes interactions between him and his parents or his school very stressful for him. Growing out of our main premise is the equally important principle that any one method of treatment cannot solve all the problems that face the child who is maladjusted in school or in the home.

The research that serves as background for the content of this book was originally planned to increase understanding of the emotionally disturbed child at school, but the findings made it obvious that they related to maladjustment of all kinds. These findings had marked implications for the diagnostic and treatment programs that were being offered by community agencies, both mental health centers and schools.

Traditionally, maladjusted or emotionally disturbed behavior has been viewed as resulting from the impact of an adverse environment—poor child management, conflict at home, lack of love—on a child during significant phases of development. Such experiences are considered primary causative factors; their effect is shown when the child alters his perception of himself and others, experiences undue anxiety in the process of growing up, and develops coping behaviors that are maladaptive. Except in those cases where a definitely established neurological or intellectual deficit is known, the child's capacities are considered intact and a insignificant contribution to the causative factors of the disturbed behavior.

We have developed the view that maladjusted patterns shown by some children may arise secondarily, produced by stress imposed by the normal demands of the environment upon a child whose developmentally immature skills make him unable to meet these demands. The immaturities that these children show in school and in social situations, in how they perceive their world, in how they comprehend the meaning of events, or in how they manipulate their own bodies in relationship to objects or events in their environment, play a significant role in the causative chain leading to disturbed behavior. How they are able to cope with day-to-day events influences how they are treated by others, how they interpret events in their environment, and how they perceive themselves. Such immaturities in development also affect and sometimes limit the kind and type of coping behaviors shown by these children. A child such as these we describe as the CPM child, the child with cognitive-perceptual-motor deficits.

Other workers in the fields of education and mental health are focusing interest on the CPM child under other names. By using the terms *learning disability* or *perceptual handicap*, which focus on only one aspect of the child's dysfunction, it is difficult to see how these handicapped children are similar. We wish to present a uniform approach that can assist in the understanding of the development of all these differently labeled children. In chapter 2, we shall try to describe the work of some of these others, after we have clearly defined our own focus.

Some readers will be particularly interested in the methodology of the research in this area and the statistical results of the studies. A description of the research is contained in the several reports filed with the Office of Education under the title "An Investigation of an Evaluation Method and Retraining Procedures for Emotionally Handicapped Children with Cognitive-Motor Deficits" (Project no. 7-01319). A summary of this material will be found in chapter 2, but for the practitioner primarily interested in the concept of the CPM child and methods of identification, evaluation, and intervention,

chapters 3 to 6 will be of more value. In addition, the testing procedure, reduced in size for economical administration, is presented in
the appendices and may serve as a manual for examiners.

This book is a distillation and summary of several years of research conducted by an interdisciplinary team working both in a
psychiatric institute and in a public school system. Contributions
from psychology, special education, and occupational therapy have
been integrated into the theory as well as into the practical programs. We offer this report at this time, not because we feel that we
have the definitive answer but because we regard our ideas as an aid
to those who want to put into practice the results of research and
bring back to research the results of practice, so that improvements
and corrections can be made in all efforts directed toward improving the chances of children to grow toward independence with a
minimum of negative experience to distort the course of their development.

# acknowledgments

From the very beginning of this project, the authors had the assistance of many individuals, who were involved in the planning, execution, and interpretation phases, and now wish to recognize their contributions. In the original planning Charles D. Beall and Norris Mottley were extremely helpful; the testing program was carried out in a most efficient manner by the following psychological examiners: Hannah Honeyman, Marilyn Wienner, Jean Levis, Marianne Crane, Dorothy Medalie, and Beryl Ax, who served as coordinator of this part. The immense job of statistical analysis was ably performed by Patricia Levin and Elaine Tsao under the direction of the head of the Computing Lab, Dr. James Grisell. Of the others who assisted with this task, we acknowledge the help of Babette Bleifeld, Susan Hayden, and Christopher Rubin.

We are especially indebted to members of the project staff: Teachers, Mary Olenik, Gayle Benson, and Arthur Wohl; Teacher aides, Joyce Lew, Gloria Miller, and Adrienne Yourist; Teacher substitute, Marianne Crane. We are also grateful for the excellent and reliable job of data collection performed by: Interviewer, Sally Ross; Psychological examiners, Louis Cohen, William Galvin, Hermine Krause, Sara Lee Silvers, Irene Stein, and Marilyn Wienner; Optometrists, Drs. Max Honeyman and Donald Lakin. We appreciate the cooperation we received from Special Education teachers of the Wyandotte Public Schools, Marcus Betwee and Susan Tenorio, and their assistance in the teacher workshop. Many people from the Lafayette Clinic business office and professional staff provided invaluable assistance.

*Acknowledgments*

We are grateful to the Board of Education of the Roseville Public Schools and Carl Brablec, Superintendent, for their cooperation; to Margaret Bronson, Assistant Superintendent, whose assistance and support was outstanding; to the principals of the individual schools, to the many teachers who gave of their time in filling out the numerous forms and rating scales; and to the members of the Beulah Baptist Church, Roseville, especially the minister, Rev. Harold Moran, and janitor, Gil Rugh, for providing the use of their church school.

Opal Barylski was our project secretary from the first and was an invaluable aid in the tremendous task of organizing materials and preparing forms and reports. Mildred Jackson and others from the Northeast Guidance Center were very helpful in the preparation of the final manuscript. Harriet Rubin provided invaluable support throughout the project.

We wish to thank the director of the Lafayette Clinic, Dr. Jacques S. Gottlieb, for his continued support, the many other members of the staff, and finally, the parents and children involved for their cooperation.

E.Z.R.
J.B.
G.B.
L.L.

# chapter one

# THE CPM CHILD

## Who Is the CPM Child?

Anyone who has worked with children professionally has met a child with cognitive-perceptual-motor deficits and probably been puzzled by him. Whether in a classroom, a club, a play group, or a clinic, there is frequently a child who cannot seem to learn, to follow the rules, to behave acceptably so he can have a good time. It is tempting to look critically at such a child's parents, wondering why his mother is not helping. It is also tempting to think that if only this child could receive psychotherapeutic help, all would be well with him.

The aspect of such a child is puzzling because he frequently seems to be above average intelligence, even though he cannot master academic subjects, and yet he behaves the same after a program of psychotherapy as he did before. It was this latter observation that led the Lafayette Clinic group to look more closely at the inpatient children who seemed to show little profit from their individual therapy. In symptomatology, the behaviors—or misbehaviors—that get the CPM child into trouble with other people, cannot differentiate him from other emotionally disturbed children. He is impulsive, he is too timid or too aggressive, he is destructive, he is apt to cry easily, he may lie, steal, urinate or defecate in his clothes, he is dependent upon others to keep him on time or in the place he should be. And, whatever his other symptoms, he is almost universally described as being an underachiever in school, that is, he functions academically at a level below expectancy, when expectancy is based on his measured intelligence.

When we attempt to formulate a description of the CPM child that will differentiate him, upon inspection, from the so-called emotionally disturbed child, we must then necessarily fail. Our thesis is that the CPM child *is* an emotionally disturbed child; he arrived at this maladaptive approach to life by a different route than the child without CPM deficits.

## Primary and Secondary Disturbance

When a child has a life history of rejection by his parents, of severely inconsistent or nonsupportive handling, of failure to receive the love, socializing experiences, and stimulation that are necessary for personality growth, we suspect that his symptomatic behavior is the result of his poor environment and that he has a primary emotional disturbance. However, when we have a child in whom the inadequate handling by the parents appears to be a result of their attempts to adjust to "something different" in this child—his clumsiness, slowness in learning to dress himself, vagueness about time and space concepts, short attention span, hyperactivity, low tolerance for frustration and associability, for a few examples—when we find that the parents for many years have been uneasy about how to handle this child and that, upon examination, the child has identifiable cognitive-perceptual-motor deficits, we feel that the emotional disturbance this child manifests is better understood as a secondary phenomenon, that it is the result of his inability to cope with the everyday demands of the environment and to perform at the same level as his peers in many activities. A child may have both, of course, a primary emotional disturbance and CPM deficits. The problem of determining this is a complex one and requires a thorough understanding of the concepts of primary emotional disturbance, secondary emotional disturbance, and CPM deficits. How this mixed picture differs from the one presented by the CPM child is not within the scope of this book. The outward behavior is the same for the child with primary emotional disturbance and for the CPM child with a secondary emotional disturbance, and this behavior is just as difficult for the environment to accept or tolerate, especially since it means that the child who has lived with these difficulties into several unrewarding school years has probably incorporated a maladaptive life style into his personality structure.

## Prolonged Dependency and Overprotection

To understand the CPM child it is important to recognize that underlying the maladaptive behaviors are skill deficiencies and, because of them, his vulnerability to environmental stress experiences is greater than that of the intact child. The CPM child is often unable to follow verbal instructions, to express his thoughts clearly, to manipulate table utensils, to remember game rules, to know left from right, or to perceive visual similarities and differences. The world is less well organized and less clearly structured for him. He is therefore more dependent upon adults to help him find his way in the world and, when the mother meets his needs by offering this extra support, structure, and protection, his observable immaturity leads people to assume that the mother is interfering with his growth by "coddling" him. His poor foundation skills also make him unable to take advantage of experiential opportunities available to him. As a result, such a child has less practice than the normal child in the very areas in which he most needs practice. Question a mother about the preschool activities of the CPM child with poor fine motor control, for example, "Could he color within the lines of a coloring book?" and she will say that he never liked to color but used to scribble so that she and her husband usually gave him trucks or other large muscle toys to play with.

## Parental Behaviors

Another striking aspect of the CPM child is that he frequently belongs to a family in which it is extremely difficult to identify the pathology. Obviously, it is possible to go into any family and find that the parents are doing something that is not ideal. Many of the CPM children, however, seem to have stable homes with interested, concerned parents who have been highly successful with their other children. The climate in the home is not observably different from that in the house of normal children, except that the difficulties the

CPM child presents have aroused so much anxiety and self-doubt in the parents that the atmosphere is often tense. And the symptomatic behavior of the CPM child has strained the parents' ability to make adjustments in their handling of him.

## Avoidance of Stress

Failure to function adequately in some areas and the negative feedback he receives when he attempts such activities lead a child to avoid difficult activities altogether, so that he does not get as much practice as the average child, and his resultant skills are even lower than they need to be. In dynamic terms, it might be said that his psychic energy goes into avoidance instead of into practice. There is a growing body of evidence which suggests that avoidance of stress in such handicapped individuals may lead to the ultimate in avoidance—psychosis (Goldfarb, 1963; Eisenberg, 1957). Now that CPM areas are being examined more frequently, it is striking to note that many teen-age psychotic patients appear to have been children with CPM deficits who could no longer tolerate the strain of trying to compete with inadequate equipment.

## Low Self-Esteem and Low Motivation

The presence of these deficits leads not only to misinterpretations of the child's abilities by others in the environment but also to a major direct impact on the direction of the child's personality development. At every stage in his development, the child sees himself as unable to cope with simple tasks; his need to depend upon his parents and other adults prevents him from achieving the kind of mastery that contributes to positive personality growth. It is a psychological truism that each success in meeting a challenge adds to the individual's confidence that he can conquer the next challenge that arises. The child with CPM deficits either fails to meet challenges or avoids being confronted by them; while other children are shouting, "Look how high I can jump." "Look at the picture I drew." "Look how fast I can ride my bike." "Look how many words I can spell," the deficient child can only offer the fact of his existence as a reason for being loved and admired. It is not surprising, then, that these children typically present themselves in negative fashion. They describe themselves as "lazy" or "stupid" or "too little to do that." The less they attempt, the less they can do, and perhaps the most striking aspect of their personality makeup as they get older is an almost total absence of motivation or achievement strivings in socially approved areas, such as school or sports.

## Recognizing versus Identifying the CPM Child

Observation and description alone are not sufficient to determine whether a child has a primary or a secondary emotional disturbance as a reaction to CPM deficits. Our postulate is that deficits in certain functions may lead to disability in learning and to disorders in behavior but that predictions from observed disabilities to pathology are not possible at the present time. The effort by many educators and psychologists to arrive at a cookbook of relationships, i.e., poor reader means undeveloped perceptual skills, fails to take into account the child as a total personality and the reason he is unsuccessful at the reading task. While we have thought of these skills as "intervening variables," what we are talking about may also be subsumed under the concept of "ego strength," as the adaptive abilities of the intellect play a large role in the individual's view of himself and in his coping mechanisms in response to environmental stress. Whatever the theoretical formulation, the major point is that the symptoms displayed by a child do not explain etiology of difficulties; it cannot be emphasized strongly enough that it is necessary to look at the organism, the quality of the development of the entire range of skills, and to examine the expectations of the home and the school. It is the appraisal of these interactions, not the symptoms of failure, that tell the story of causation. Similarly, the presence of negative attitudes in the home or other evidences of potentially stressful circumstances do not presume an environmentally determined disturbance. Any disturbance in adjustment may be viewed as a function of both immediate and remote antecedents. With some conditions, especially primary emotional disturbance, the remote antecedents, such as early environmental attitudes, are the more significant and without understanding; dealing with these, no improvement can be expected. On the other hand, with secondary emotional disorders, stress at home and at school interacting with CPM deficits is the major determinant of the deviant behavior, and both settings require adaptations for improved adjustment.

For us, then, a diagnostic evaluation consists of an adequate assessment of cognitive-perceptual-motor skills as well as of motivational state, capabilities for attention and concentration coupled with an evaluation of potential stress factors at home or at school. In school, these may consist of the demands of the learning task, the classroom environment, or the teacher's style; at home, the expectations for achievement, the parental understanding of the child's development, and the stability of the family.

The child's malfunctioning in this way is understood in terms of the dynamic interaction of organismic factors with environmental forces. With the CPM child, the differentiating feature is the presence of deficits in cognitive, perceptual, or motor functioning.

## Why Identify?

In many situations, it may be possible to identify CPM deficits in the disturbed child and to recognize quite clearly that his symptomatic behavior does indeed represent a secondary emotional disturbance. The question might be properly asked: So what? The evidence is not clear that all of these deficits can be overcome through training; it is not certain that improvement in areas of deficit does generalize to academic achievement, and many school systems or localities do not have the facilities for appropriate retraining and remedial programs. Is there any purpose in examining children with a CPM battery?

One major purpose for defining CPM dysfunction is to indicate the need to relieve stress. Recognition of the role of stress in the persistence of maladaptive behaviors and the manner in which retarded development in some areas leads a child to find stressful experiences which may be exhilarating to the intact child have important implications for school people, parents, and mental health practitioners. Such recognition inevitably requires that: (1) a comprehensive evaluation be made of the current school functioning of the child; (2) the sources of maladjustment be identified; (3) remedial approaches be developed to improve functioning; and (4) guidelines be provided for parents and teachers to reduce immediate stress around the child. When the parents or teacher recognize that the environment influences the child's failure to perform in the classroom or to adjust to life situations and such inability is not just the fault of the child, a therapeutic value is achieved, especially if it leads the school and home to provide the kind of challenges that are within the success level of the child.

Planning an effective program to improve a child's skills is another major resultant of the comprehensive evaluation. (Here, assessment of CPM skill functioning is essential.) Intervention may take several forms but they all must be based on knowledge of the level of the child in skills, academics, and, ideally, dynamics.

## The Typical CPM Child—Does He Exist?

Although we may ask, Does the typical CPM child exist? it is not possible to give a composite picture of him that will apply to all such children. By now, it is clear that he is not identified by particular symptomatic behavior. He usually has more than one skill deficit which may be in auditory as well as visual perception, in integration and conceptual skills, in fine motor control or gross motor abilities. He is usually at least within the "average" range of intelligence and this leads to expectations on the part of the school for achievement that he generally does not and cannot accomplish. In our experience, it has not been unusual to see such children with very superior I.Q.s, ranging as high as 139 on the Wechsler Intelligence Scale for Children; in such cases the bewilderment of the school is understandable. Occasionally these children also exhibit extremely high achievement in one area, such as reading, but cannot control their behavior appropriately and cannot begin to perform the simplest arithmetic operations. Again the apparent contradictions make the child a puzzle to school and parent observers.

The multiplicity of possible symptoms and the infinite combinations of possible skill deficits determine that our major thesis is that all children should receive a thorough assessment in the areas that appear related both to academic achievement and to successful coping with the environment. Other workers, such as Maslow (1967), deHirsch (1966); and Silver, Hagan, and Hersch (1965),whose primary aim has been the development of remediation methods, have also moved in the direction of a comprehensive assessment rather than a single-test approach.

## Early Identification

In nearly all cases of children who come to the attention of the special services in school, in the clinic, or with the private practitioner, there is an early history of problems. A kindergarten teacher has observed "immaturity," and other teachers have reported inappropriate or anomalous behavior in the early grades. By the time the child reaches the upper elementary years—by the time, that is, that someone has decided to stop waiting for him to outgrow whatever ails him—there has been a serious negative effect upon his personality development. Overcoming this pattern of avoidance and denial is a major task for the teacher entrusted with planning a remedial program for such a child; there is no way of making up completely for the several years during which he has failed to acquire and practice skills that his peers have been developing in themselves in that time. For that reason, we urge that a program of CPM skill assessment be developed for use with kindergarten and first grade children wherever possible. However this approach has demonstrated usefulness even with upper elementary and older school children.

# chapter two

# HISTORICAL BACKGROUND

Leton (1967) described in 1960 what he called "a new problem in the field of special education," i.e., atypical children confronting in the classroom teacher. He described the problem in the following terms:

> There is a sizeable group of exceptional children for whom no adequate educational facilities exist. These are children who have incurred a mild neurological impairment and as a result, may have severe learning disabilities or may exhibit behavior deviations which make adjustment in the regular classroom difficult, even though their intelligence scores are within the range for "normal."

Leton's "new" problem turns out to be one that is currently attracting considerable attention but is not really new. As early as 1947, Strauss and Lehtinen (1947) focused attention on brain injured children and the need for a specialized educational approach with them.

Since 1947, a number of workers have recognized the child who fails to learn, who has minimal neurological findings, but is noteworthy because of his clumsiness, inattentiveness, poor concentration, and general disruptiveness. However, a great deal of confusion has existed in regard to the diagnosis of such a child. Depending on the training, professional discipline, philosophy, or particular bias, workers may have labeled him brain injured, emotionally disturbed, or mentally retarded. With advances in diagnostic methodology, a variety of other labels have also been applied. In reviewing the dilemma facing educators in this field, Dunn (1965) listed twenty-three different terms used to describe this undefined condition. Clements (1966) reported a total of thirty-eight terms that he found in the literature used to describe the child. The assumption of those who apply the label is that individuals in a group share commonalities that are not shared by those who are not so labeled. Unfortunately, this has failed to be demonstrated. In an attempt to resolve this confusion, the Task Force on Terminology and Identification of the National Institute of Neurological Diseases and Blindness and the National Society for Crippled Children and Adults, Inc., chose the term "minimal brain dysfunction" as best representing this syndrome, reflecting by this term an obvious medical bias. The United States Office of Education, in cooperation with the Council for Exceptional Children, selected the term "major learning disorder," reflecting its particular concern with those who are educationally handicapped. These last two approaches do recognize a more general syndrome and avoid the pitfall of specificity of such terms as *perceptual disorder* or *hyperkinetic child*. The fault of the first is the implicit assumption about etiology; of the second, a focus on only one specific result of the problems these children manifest.

We employ a descriptive terminology that recognizes the varied symptoms presented by this disordered child. Major emphasis is on a faulty developmental process that may manifest itself in behavioral disturbance or learning disorder, with or without recognizable clinical signs of brain damage. The antecedent conditions are unclear and vary from case to case, but include the possibilities of prenatal, birth, or postnatal trauma, environmental understimulation, genetic factors, or some other aberration of development not yet understood.

From our research and from the findings consistently and repeatedly reported by others it clearly emerges that, in the group of children under discussion, some dysfunction in cognitive-perceptual-motor skills is noted. For this reason, we have chosen to initiate our investigation with the construction of methods that among those who are maladapted, can adequately identify those who show a pattern of cognitive-perceptual-motor skills that is significantly deviant from that seen in other children, including those who are not maladapted either in behavior or in learning.

24

# table 1

## Cognitive-Perceptual-Motor Functions

| Function | Definition |
|---|---|
| 1. Visual perception | Central response to visual stimulus, inferred from verbal or motor response |
| a. Fine discrimination | Recognition of similarities and differences when the stimuli—presented visually—are increasingly similar, checked along various dimensions including form, size and space |
| b. Constancy | Holding of a symbolic representation of a form, in both simple and complex stimulus situations |
| 2. Auditory perception | Central response to auditory stimulus inferred from verbal or motor response |
| a. Fine discrimination | Recognition of similarities and differences between auditorily presented stimuli; not musical sounds, but, rather, language symbols |
| b. Constancy | Holding of an auditory stimulus and recognition of it among competing stimuli |
| 3. Memory | Recall of visual and auditory stimuli |
| a. Immediate rote | Recall of digits or unrelated series of items, immediately following presentation |
| b. Immediate meaningful | Recall of rote details, content and meaning, immediately after presentation |
| c. Delayed | Recall of rote details, after time lapse |
| 4. Orientation | Awareness of relationships between oneself and events and objects in the environment, along the dimensions of time, space and size |
| 5. Integration | Ability to combine discrete tangible stimuli into meaningful whole |
| a. Non-verbal | Ability to abstract qualities or meanings from stimuli and to form constructs transferable from situation to situation, using materials that are tangible, abstract or numerical |
| b. Symbolic | Abstraction of meaning from written or oral material that is suggested by the content but not explicitly stated |
| c. Inferential reasoning | |
| 6. Linguistics | |
| a. Input | Ability to understand what is said and to demonstrate formation of habits of language in keeping with construction of English |
| b. Output | Communication and expression of ideas either through gestures or words |
| 7. Fine motor control | Control of fine movements in simple and complex situations |
| 8. Gross motor coordination | Coordination of large muscles in purposeful manner, including eye-hand coordination, extremities and proprioception |
| a. Eye-hand | Use of large muscles to perform coordinated tasks |
| b. Extremities | Smooth functioning of arms & legs |
| 9. Tactile-kinesthetic proprioceptive perception | Central response to stimuli presented only to tactual senses—inferred from motor and verbal responses |
| | Utilization of information from large muscles for central balance |

Assuming that development could proceed at different rates for differing skills, a testing program was designed to cover a broad range of skills. One such set of skills involved perceptual discrimination—visual, auditory, tactile, and kinesthetic. The question asked here is: How well is the child able to make perceptual discriminations, checking on the input process. The abilities to abstract and generalize, to remember and make associations or inferences are other aspects of cognitive functioning measured. Finally, we incorporated measures of fine and gross coordination, including combinations of input and output, such as eye-hand coordination. In this way, a comprehensive assessment of cognitive-perceptual-motor skills was accomplished. A summary of the nine CPM areas defined for measurement is described in table 1.

In our first major study, upon which part of this book is based, we found deviant cognitive-perceptual-motor patterns associated with 40 percent of behaviorally maladjusted children in one public school system. In this study, which utilized a comprehensive battery of both standardized and new tests covering nine different areas of CPM functioning, 400 children were examined, 100 from each of the first, second, third, and fifth grades in the Roseville, Michigan, Public Schools. At each grade level, half of the children demonstrated gross evidences of behavior maladjustment according to a behavior checklist filled out by the classroom teachers (see chapter 3); the other half were essentially problem-free (as defined by an absence of behavior maladjustment observable to the teacher). The distribution of subjects by sex, age, I.Q., and grade is shown in table 2. This part compared the performance of the behaviorally maladjusted children on cognitive, perceptual, and motor tasks with children who were problem-free.

The measure used to compare these two groups was the CPM dysfunction score, a composite measure based on the total number of tests on which the child scored below an established criterion. Only those measures that discriminated significantly between maladjusted and problem-free children were used to derive this composite score. The criterion was a cutting score based on a score one standard deviation below the mean for the total grade sample for each test.

## table 2

## *Distribution of Sex, Age, I.Q., and Achievement for All Grades*

### Mean Scores for Grades and Groups

|  | Grade 1 | | Grade 2 | | Grade 3 | | Grade 5 | |
|---|---|---|---|---|---|---|---|---|
|  | Exp. | Cont. | Exp. | Cont. | Exp. | Cont. | Exp. | Cont. |
| Males | 30 | 30 | 30 | 30 | 29 | 30 | 30 | 30 |
| Females | 20 | 20 | 19 | 20 | 20 | 20 | 20 | 20 |
| Total No. | 50 | 50 | 49 | 50 | 49 | 50 | 50 | 50 |
| Age (mos.) | 80.7 | 82.3 | 96.5 | 94.6 | 107.3 | 105.5 | 129.8 | 126.5 † |
| WISC IQ | | | | | | | | |
| Verbal | 96.1 | 106.9 † | 97.3 | 107.3 † | 98.6 | 104.2 * | 101.2 | 112.0 † |
| Perform. | 103.2 | 113.3 † | 99.8 | 113.0 † | 99.3 | 110.1 * | 102.9 | 112.9 † |
| Full scale | 99.4 | 110.8 † | 98.3 | 111.0 † | 98.8 | 107.6 † | 102.3 | 113.5 † |
| Met. Achiev. | | | | | | | | |
| Av. Gr. Ach.‡ | −.22 | +.31 † | −.26 | +.59 † | +.04 | .92 † | −.63 | .55 † |

\* .05
† .01
‡ This score was derived from the Average Grade Achievement score of the Metropolitan Achievement Test and represents the discrepancy between test grade achievement and chronological age grade placement.

A comparison of the two groups indicated significant differences between a subgroup of the maladjusted children which was both below the average of that group and below the entire problem-free group in CPM functioning. These results, presented in table 3 and in figure 1, indicate a clear differentiation of the subgroup of the maladjusted subjects who show significant evidences of cognitive-perceptual-motor dysfunction.

The study revealed that 40 percent of the maladjusted subjects showed severe CPM dysfunction, a finding which was consistent in all four grades studied. In a recent study Mora et al. (1968) reported similar results when children from a residential treatment-center population were examined by a pediatric neurological battery which included, in addition to some of the traditional neurological tests, measures of perceptual motor function, gross motor coordination, orientation, memory and language function.

Our findings also indicated a high correlation between CPM def-

## table 3

### Comparison of Maladjusted and Problem-Free Groups on Number of Error Scores Above and Below Criterion

| | Number of Subjects | | | |
|---|---|---|---|---|
| | Maladjusted | | Problem-Free | |
| Grade | $\lesssim 6$ | $\gtrsim 6$ | $\lesssim 6$ | $\gtrsim 6$ |
| 1 | 30 | 20 | 50 | 0 |
| 2 | 25 | 24 | 48 | 2 |
| 3 | 29 | 20 | 49 | 1 |
| Grade | $\lesssim 5$ | $\gtrsim 5$ | $\lesssim 5$ | $\gtrsim 5$ |
| 5 | 29 | 21 | 50 | 0 |

icits and learning retardation. Although the subjects for this study were originally identified on the basis of behavioral maladjustment, achievement testing revealed a startling percentage of subjects with academic learning problems. In grades one, two, three, and five, 70, 75, 65, and 80 percent of the maladjusted group were below expectancy. In the control (problem-free) groups, 14 to 28 percent were below grade (see table 4). However, the majority of those maladjusted subjects with below grade functioning were those with high CPM dysfunction (see table 5). For grades one, two, three, and five,

## table 4

### Comparison of Maladjusted and Problem-Free Groups on Average Grade Achievement *

| | Maladjusted | | | | Problem-Free | | | |
|---|---|---|---|---|---|---|---|---|
| | Total | Cases Below Grade | | | Total | Cases Below Grade | | |
| Grade | N | Male | Female | Total | N | Male | Female | Total |
| 1 | 50 | 26 (87) | 9 (45) | 35 (70) | 50 | 5 (17) | 6 (30) | 11 (22) |
| 2 | 49 | 24 (80) | 13 (65) | 37 (76) | 50 | 10 (33) | 4 (20) | 14 (28) |
| 3 | 49 | 19 (63) | 13 (65) | 32 (65) | 50 | 7 (23) | 0 (0) | 7 (14) |
| 5 | 50 | 24 (80) | 16 (80) | 40 (80) | 50 | 7 (23) | 3 (33) | 10 (20) |

* Discrepancy score.

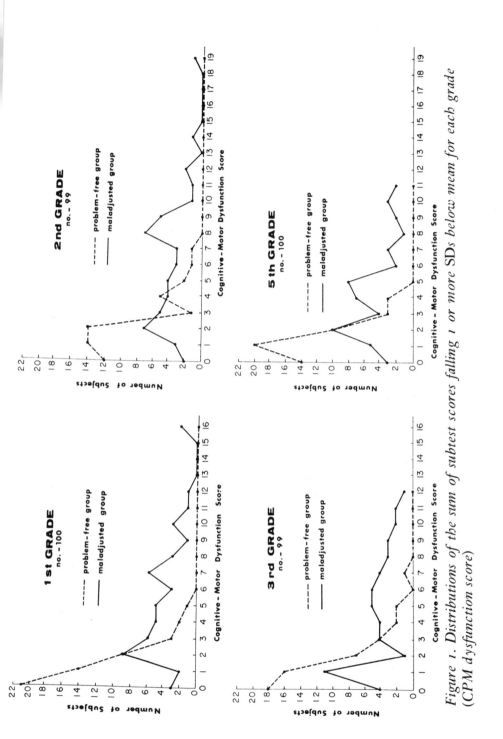

Figure 1. Distributions of the sum of subtest scores falling 1 or more SDs below mean for each grade (CPM dysfunction score)

## table 6 *Behavior Checklist*

*Instructions:* Place *one* check mark in the margin opposite those items which are representative of this child's typical behavior. Use *two* check marks for those items which he shows more frequently. Use *three* check marks if the behavior item is most outstanding by its frequency.

*N.B.* The rater should be very familiar with the child's classroom behavior over a period of time. Take the average child in a regular classroom as your basis for comparions.

NAME:_____ SEX: ____ BIRTH DATE:_____ GRADE:_____

DATE:_____ TEACHER:_____

1. Very sensitive to criticism.
2. Expresses feelings of inadequacy about self.
3. Never makes self known to others.
4. Is excessively neat or finicky about work or possessions.
5. Overconforms to rules.
6. Aggressive in underhanded ways.
7. Seeks attention excessively.
8. Very short attention span.
9. Can't work independently.
10. Shows signs of nervousness (nailbiting, crying, tics, rocking).
11. Overly preoccupied with sexual matters.
12. Daydreams.
13. Seems to fear being assertive even in ordinary ways (asking to go to toilet, defending self, making legitimate messes, joining in allowable noisy play).
14. Is receiving, or recommended, speech correction.
15. Poor coordination (trouble with buttoning, tying shoes, getting shoes on correct feet).
16. Can't take turns: "Me first."
17. Lacks responsibility for self, always has excuse for shortcomings.
18. Resists limits or rules in group games.
19. Tendencies toward enuresis or soiling of clothing.
20. Very messy with work or belongings.
21. Negativistic: "I won't."
22. Difficulty in handling working materials, such as crayons, scissors, paste, etc.
23. Considered an isolate in class.
24. Engages in much solitary play.
25. Displays infantile behavior (crawling, whining, clinging, sucking, chewing, etc.).
26. Makes odd noises.
27. Makes irrelevant or inappropriate remarks.
28. Misinterprets simple statements.
29. Is disoriented in space; is confused as to directions given.
30. Shows excessive fantasy preoccupation.
31. Tendencies toward primitive hostilities, temper tantrums, wild destruction.
32. Holds back in free play.
33. Antisocial tendencies (steals, lies, destroys property, bullies, defies, resents discipline).
34. Frequently tardy, frequently absent.
35. Poorly cared for before leaving for school.
36. Easily fatigued.
37. Often ill; other physical problems.
38. Feigns illness.
39. In academic area, evidence of underachievement, or overachievement, in relation to ability.

Eli Z. Rubin, Clyde Simson, and Marcus Betwee, *Emotionally Handicapped Children and the Elementary School*. Wayne State University Press, 1966.

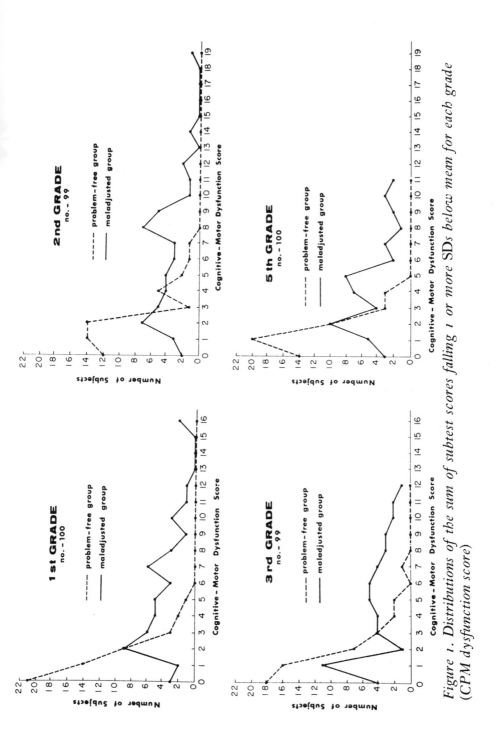

Figure 1. Distributions of the sum of subtest scores falling 1 or more SDs below mean for each grade (CPM dysfunction score)

## table 5

### Comparison of High and Low Dysfunction Groups on Average Grade Achievement *

Number and Percent of Subjects

| Grade | HIGH DYSFUNCTION | | | | | | LOW DYSFUNCTION | | | | | |
|---|---|---|---|---|---|---|---|---|---|---|---|---|
| | Number Cases | | | Below Grade | | | Number Cases | | | Below Grade | | |
| | M | F | Σ | M | F | Σ | M | F | Σ | M | F | Σ |
| 1 | 16 | 4 | 20 | 16 (100) | 4 (100) | 20 (100) | 14 | 16 | 30 | 9 (64) | 5 (31) | 14 (47) |
| 2 | 17 | 7 | 24 | 15 (88) | 5 (71) | 20 (83) | 13 | 12 | 25 | 5 (38) | 7 (58) | 12 (48) |
| 3 | 14 | 6 | 20 | 11 (55) | 6 (30) | 17 (85) | 15 | 14 | 29 | 9 (60) | 7 (50) | 16 (55) |
| 5† | 14 | 7 | 21 | 13 (93) | 5 (71) | 18 (86) | 16 | 13 | 29 | 10 (63) | 10 (77) | 20 (69) |

* Discrepancy score.
† High dysfunction = $\geq$ 5.

100, 83, 85, and 86 percent of the high dysfunction subjects were functioning below grade expectancy. Of the low dysfunction subjects, 47, 48, 55, and 69 percent from these four grades were below grade in academic functioning. Although it is apparent, then, that there is a strong association of academic retardation with behavior maladjustment, the stronger association is between high CPM dysfunction and academic retardation. These findings emphasize the importance of identifying high dysfunction subjects for remedial intervention; they form the basis in part for the second phase of our research program that was directed toward evaluating methods of remediation for children with cognitive-perceptual-motor deficits. In this instance, too, the learning disorder has been viewed as a result of limitations in specific skills that make a child unable to profit from particular types of academic instruction.

We describe the children we found not as emotionally disturbed, or as brain damaged, or as children with learning disorders, but as children with developmental deficits in cognitive-perceptual-motor skills. Our methods lead naturally to the development of a descriptive profile of variations in performance on a set of tasks that reflect a comprehensive range of skills.

# chapter three

# EVALUATION OF CPM DYSFUNCTION

## Identifying Children for Testing

Not all emotionally disturbed children have cognitive-perceptual-motor deficits. A teacher cannot diagnose this condition when she sees restless, inattentive behavior with slow learning. The child psychiatrist cannot make this judgment from his observation of anxious behavior with low frustration tolerance, impulsivity, or evidences of low self-image, or from the history, even if it is revealed that there were some difficulties in the prenatal, birth, or early developmental period. The neurologist, also, cannot diagnose this condition from his examination or from the results of the EEG.

Yet in understanding any behavior disturbance, an important first step is to determine whether or not CPM dysfunction is a significant element. It is essential to be able to differentiate the CPM child from others who do not have such developmental deficits. We make the same distinction here as Denhoff (1968) does in diagnosing a disease entity and evaluating functioning inefficiency. We may not be able to resolve the question of etiology but we can describe a condition so that relevant treatment methods can be instituted.

The first problem in our research study was to determine which children are most likely to show CPM deficits. Our previous clinical and pilot investigations and a review of the literature indicated to us that CPM dysfunction was likely to be associated with disturbed behavioral functioning and/or learning difficulties. Sometimes the teacher may observe behavior that may lead to a constructive hypothesis regarding the possibility of CPM dysfunction.

## table 6 *Behavior Checklist*

*Instructions:* Place *one* check mark in the margin opposite those items which are representative of this child's typical behavior. Use *two* check marks for those items which he shows more frequently. Use *three* check marks if the behavior item is most outstanding by its frequency.

*N.B.* The rater should be very familiar with the child's classroom behavior over a period of time. Take the average child in a regular classroom as your basis for comparions.

NAME:_____ SEX:___ BIRTH DATE:_____ GRADE:_____

DATE:_____ TEACHER:_____

1. Very sensitive to criticism.
2. Expresses feelings of inadequacy about self.
3. Never makes self known to others.
4. Is excessively neat or finicky about work or possessions.
5. Overconforms to rules.
6. Aggressive in underhanded ways.
7. Seeks attention excessively.
8. Very short attention span.
9. Can't work independently.
10. Shows signs of nervousness (nailbiting, crying, tics, rocking).
11. Overly preoccupied with sexual matters.
12. Daydreams.
13. Seems to fear being assertive even in ordinary ways (asking to go to toilet, defending self, making legitimate messes, joining in allowable noisy play).
14. Is receiving, or recommended, speech correction.
15. Poor coordination (trouble with buttoning, tying shoes, getting shoes on correct feet).
16. Can't take turns: "Me first."
17. Lacks responsibility for self, always has excuse for shortcomings.
18. Resists limits or rules in group games.
19. Tendencies toward enuresis or soiling of clothing.
20. Very messy with work or belongings.
21. Negativistic: "I won't."
22. Difficulty in handling working materials, such as crayons, scissors, paste, etc.
23. Considered an isolate in class.
24. Engages in much solitary play.
25. Displays infantile behavior (crawling, whining, clinging, sucking, chewing, etc.).
26. Makes odd noises.
27. Makes irrelevant or inappropriate remarks.
28. Misinterprets simple statements.
29. Is disoriented in space; is confused as to directions given.
30. Shows excessive fantasy preoccupation.
31. Tendencies toward primitive hostilities, temper tantrums, wild destruction.
32. Holds back in free play.
33. Antisocial tendencies (steals, lies, destroys property, bullies, defies, resents discipline).
34. Frequently tardy, frequently absent.
35. Poorly cared for before leaving for school.
36. Easily fatigued.
37. Often ill; other physical problems.
38. Feigns illness.
39. In academic area, evidence of underachievement, or overachievement, in relation to ability.

Eli Z. Rubin, Clyde Simson, and Marcus Betwee, *Emotionally Handicapped Children and the Elementary School.* Wayne State University Press, 1966.

Mrs. Smith, a first grade teacher, noted that John was able to respond verbally, participate fully in class discussion, but was slow to complete written work. His efforts with written work were laborious and painful and the results were messy and illegible. Rarely was he able to finish an assignment. His behavior during this classroom activity was marked by increased restlessness and inattentiveness. She suspected some kind of eye-hand coordination problem.

Teachers' observations may reveal other outstanding characteristics that might predict some immature skill development, e.g., clumsiness, continued reversals in reading or writing, poor construction of form in drawings, or inadequacies in visual memory revealed by difficulties in copying work from board or book. These teacher observations, if directed, can provide meaningful direction for subsequent examinations.

Earlier research with a checklist of behaviors indicative of classroom maladjustment suggests an approach that can provide this direction. This instrument can also serve to support an in-service training program with the objective of improving teachers' abilities to make consistent, comprehensive, and unbiased observation of the child's classroom skills and behavior.

The Behavior Checklist (table 6) was used in our recent research to help locate subjects who might be likely to demonstrate CPM difficulties. This instrument had been used in an earlier study (Rubin, Simson, Betwee, 1966) and shown to be effective in picking out children at school who were later found to be emotionally disturbed by clinical examination. The findings from that earlier study also indicated that emotionally disturbed children in school demonstrated a high rate of behaviors that appeared to be correlated with poor functioning in a variety of cognitive, perceptual, or motor skills. A factor analysis of this checklist using a sample of eighty-four diagnosed emotionally disturbed children revealed seven major clusters. These are presented in table 7. Items from the first factor, Disorientation and Maladaptation to the Environment, were most commonly found in this sample of primary grade children. Finding poor coordination, disorientation in space, messy with work and belongings, etc., associated with behavior disturbance and learning difficulties, led to the Roseville study. The purpose of that study was to deter-

# table 7
## *Behavior Checklist Factors*

### FACTOR I
#### Disorientation and Maladaptation to the Environment

| Item | Symptom | Loading |
|---|---|---|
| 28. | Misinterprets simple statements | +.70 |
| 29. | Disoriented in space | +.70 |
| 12. | Daydreams | +.65 |
| 26. | Makes odd noises | +.63 |
| 15. | Poor coordination | +.61 |
| 8. | Short attention span | +.56 |
| 20. | Messy with work and belongings | +.56 |
| 9. | Can't work independently | +.55 |
| 27. | Makes irrelevant remarks | +.54 |
| 22. | Difficulty in handling materials | +.48 |
| 10. | Show signs of nervousness | +.41 |

### FACTOR II
#### Antisocial Behavior

| Item | Symptom | Loading |
|---|---|---|
| 31. | Tends toward primitive hostility | +.68 |
| 21. | Negativistic | +.67 |
| 2. | Feelings of inadequacy | +.48 |
| 33. | Antisocial tendencies | +.46 |

### FACTOR III
#### Unassertive, Over-conforming Behavior

| Item | Symptom | Loading |
|---|---|---|
| 13. | Fear of being assertive | +.78 |
| 32. | Holds back in free play | +.70 |
| 24. | Much solitary play | +.55 |
| 23. | Considered isolate in class | +.52 |
| 5. | Overconforms to rules | +.44 |
| 19. | Tends toward enuresis or soiling | +.44 |

### FACTOR IV
#### Neglect

| Item | Symptom | Loading |
|---|---|---|
| 34. | Frequently tardy or absent | +.74 |
| 35. | Poorly cared for before school | +.65 |
| 37. | Often ill | +.42 |

### FACTOR V
#### Infantile Behavior

| Item | Symptom | Loading |
|---|---|---|
| 25. | Displays infantile behavior | +.47 |
| 1. | Very sensitive to criticism | +.43 |
| 36. | Easily fatigued | +.43 |

### FACTOR VI
#### Immature Social Behavior

| Item | Symptom | Loading |
|---|---|---|
| 16. | Can't take turns | +.67 |
| 18. | Resists limits or rules | +.64 |
| 7. | Seeks attention excessively | +.55 |

### FACTOR VII
#### Irresponsible Behavior

| Item | Symptom | Loading |
|---|---|---|
| 6. | Aggressive in underhanded ways | +.57 |
| 17. | Lacks responsibility for self | +.53 |

### UNIQUE FACTORS

| Item | Symptom |
|---|---|
| 3. | Never makes self known |
| 4. | Excessively neat |
| 11. | Overpreoccupied with sex |
| 14. | Speech correction |
| 30. | Excessive fantasy |
| 38. | Feigns illness |
| 39. | Over or under achievement |

Eli Z. Rubin, Clyde Simson, and Marcus Betwee, *Emotionally Handicapped Children and the Elementary School*. Wayne State University Press, 1966.

mine to what degree cognitive-motor dysfunction was related to be-havior disturbance and learning disorders and to determine methods of measurement.

The Behavior Checklist was administered in this study to all children in the Roseville Public Schools from grades one, two, three, and five, a total of 4,498 children. From this population, we were then able to pick a sample of fifty very maladjusted children and fifty problem-free subjects from each grade (see table 8). Al-though we selected only those who showed the worst behavior, it can be seen from the third column in the table that there were prob-ably many others at each grade who were demonstrating behavioral

## table 8
### A Description of Behavior Checklist Ratings on the Total Population from Grades 1, 2, 3, and 5

| Grade | Total Sample | No. of Subjects 1 or More Symptoms | Problem Group 8 or More Symptoms | | Final Study Sample * | | |
|---|---|---|---|---|---|---|---|
| | | | No. | % of Total No. | No. | % of Problem Grp. | % of Total No. |
| 1 | M 659 | 468 | 82 | 12.4 | 30 | 6.4 | 4.6 |
| | F 591 | 346 | 38 | 6.4 | 20 | 5.8 | 3.4 |
| | T 1250 | 814 | 120 | | | | |
| 2 | M 562 | 369 | 82 | 14.6 | 30 | 8.1 | 5.3 |
| | F 538 | 275 | 35 | 6.5 | 20 | 7.3 | 3.7 |
| | T 1100 | 644 | 117 | | | | |
| 3 | M 545 | 358 | 56 | 10.3 | 30 | 8.4 | 5.5 |
| | F 556 | 263 | 17 | 3.1 | 20 | 7.6 | 3.6 |
| | T 1101 | 621 | 73 | | | | |
| 5 | M 527 | 322 | 49 | 9.3 | 30 | 9.3 | 5.7 |
| | F 520 | 235 | 14 | 2.7 | 20 | 8.5 | 3.8 |
| | T 1047 | 557 | 63 | | | | |
| TOTALS | 4498 | 2636 | 373 | 8.3 | 200 | 7.6 | 4.4 |

* Grade 1, 2 males — 8 or more items, 4 or more items checked 3 times
      "   3   " — 8 or more items, 3 or more items checked 3 times
      "   5   " — 8 or more items, 4 or more items checked 2 times
Grade 1, 2 females — 8 or more items, 3 or more items checked 2 times
      "   3, 5   " — 6 or more items, 3 or more items checked 2 times

difficulties. Using a criterion of eight items or more checked, we would estimate that 3 to 15 percent of the children in these grades were showing moderate to severe adjustment difficulties. In keeping with other reports, it is noteworthy that the incidence for boys exceeds that for girls in the proportion of approximately three to one in most instances.

## Behavior Checklist Procedure

By giving to the teachers in a group an introduction to the instrument which provided an opportunity to clarify the meaning of some of the items, we found that the teachers could utilize this method of selecting from their classroom those children who were having major problems. The range of items helped the teacher to focus her observations on all types of behavior, not only aggressive, antisocial, disruptive behavior but also withdrawn or overly quiet fearful adjustment.

The instructions accompanying the instrument indicated that the ratings should be made on the basis of characteristic behavior. For this reason, the teacher was asked not to fill out the form until after at least three to four weeks of observation. The instrument is not to be used to judge behavior from a single observation. Using the checklist in the manner recommended, teachers can reliably perform the first step in an aggressive screening program at any grade level that has as its aim the identification of those for whom special attention is required. Variations in this form, adapting the items for a younger age group, have been used with preschool groups including nursery schools and headstart programs.

In addition, the Behavior Checklist offers a method of communication between the teacher and the school psychologist or school social worker. It enables the teacher to pinpoint the specific symptomatic behavior displayed by a given child, helping to go beyond the vague global descriptions of "immature" or "disturbed."

## Evaluation for CPM Dysfunction

Recognition of disturbed behavior is not identical with determining CPM dysfunction. Only some of these children have CPM dysfunction. Distinctive signs are necessary in order to take the next step in the determination. In the classroom, the teacher will observe some children who are unable to attend to the work, who show maladaptive behaviors yet seem to have the ability to learn. These are the children who are the particular candidates for a CPM assessment.

## Evaluating CPM Deficit in a Mental Health Clinic

It may appear to some that to distinguish between school and clinic is an arbitrary and even an incorrect distinction to make. The assumption here, however, is that the child coming to a clinic will be more likely to be evaluated with regard to his need for treatment rather than for education. Because of the evidence that many children seen at child clinics or psychiatric hospitals do demonstrate CPM deficits, it appears appropriate to distinguish particular methods of assessment relevant to the theoretical biases and methodology characteristically employed at clinics.

It is first necessary to assume that the clinicians recognize that in some instances a faulty developmental process can be the basis for the creation of anxiety and symptomatic behavior. In the clinic examination it is necessary to establish the presence or absence of CPM deficit in order to construct the hypothesis of "secondary emotional disorder." Furthermore, the clinician will be quick to recognize that a disordered development is sufficient to create conditions that give rise to enduring deviant personality traits including such maladaptive behavior as low frustration tolerance, feelings of inadequacy, avoidance, denial, and projection mechanisms as well as a prolonged need for dependency gratification. Enduring personality characteristics must be differentiated from those behaviors, such as inattentiveness, restlessness, whining, attention-seeking, and disruptive acts, that are more likely induced situationally because of adverse parental handling or stress in the school room. In addition to the contribution of social history, the documentation of the degree of social and family pathology as a potential contributor, an evaluation must be taken of the school expectations in relation to the child's capacity. Clinical psychological examination including projectives, testing, and psychiatric examinations further contribute to this understanding.

The combining of signs from examinations with factors derived from past events suggestive of causation leads to the formulation of a clinical diagnosis. Treatment procedures relevant to the cause are generally preferred, although, in the absence of clear definition of etiology, symptomatic treatment is often recommended. In this model, it is important to utilize examination procedures to establish the presence of CPM deficit as a demonstrable component of the child's functioning. Recognizing that the behavioral syndrome is the final result of this causative chain and that it has possibly been complicated by parental handling techniques as well as school pressures, the clinician is directed to employ a multipronged treatment program best characterized as psycho-educational.

## The Testing Procedure

It is not intended that a CPM battery be a substitute for other psychological measures. This assessment is most meaningful in the context of a total psychological evaluation which includes a full scale evaluation of intellectual and personality factors, including projective materials, such as the Rorschach, the Thematic Apperception Test, and Draw a Family or Draw a Person. Even in instances where it is clear that the principal problem is uneven development —with specific CPM limitations—the projective materials help to delineate the degree to which the difficulties in coping have distorted personality development. At times, they indicate that some emotional problems are present which have developed independently of the other difficulties and, at other times, they reveal that the stress on the child has resulted in massive ego disruption to the point of psychosis. Obviously, planning of a therapeutic or remedial program for any child must be influenced by the findings of these projective materials.

There is some tendency among educators and psychologists to ignore these measures completely, because of the limitations of the intelligence test in prediction of school success. However, in making maximum use of the CPM battery and planning remedial techniques, the intelligence test is a valuable tool. The obtained I.Q. is one important way of gauging the degree to which developmental unevenness and CPM deficits have interfered with the total intellectual development, or to put it another way, the degree to which the child has been able to make use of areas of strength in achieving a given intellectual level. Additionally, it appears on the basis of *present experience* that the obtained I.Q. is helpful in determining the ceiling which may be reached by an individual child with the benefit of remedial intervention. A child of above average I.Q. will, it appears, make greater eventual gains as a result of intervention than will a child with the same level of CPM functioning but with a dull-normal or borderline I.Q.

It is because of the necessity for interrelating the findings of many aspects of the evaluation that leads us to recommend that the battery be employed by a psychologist—either a clinical psychologist or an educational psychologist who has had experience with projective techniques. Administration of the CPM battery may be done by nonprofessional people, if they have been carefully trained, but the interpretation of the results is the responsibility of a professional person experienced in the use of intelligence tests and projective materials.

## The Lafayette Clinic CPM Battery

One of the difficulties in the development of instruments adequate for measuring CPM deficits is that the selection of such instruments depends on the goal of measurement. The psychiatric clinic has heretofore necessarily been interested in interpersonal variables: how well a given child relates to other people. The school has been interested in whether a child has the equipment to learn to read and has taken the view that the I.Q. could answer that question. The opportunity to average out scores on various tests—such as the Wechsler Intelligence Scale for Children—and arrive at a composite score enabled many practitioners to ignore intra-individual differences that frequently pointed to existing deficits in the child. Again, the composite intelligence test score, having been used as the basis for expectancy, allowed the school to say that, since the child was at least average in intelligence and therefore had the ability to learn, failure to achieve must be due to something like an "emotional

# table 9
## Tests That Discriminate between Maladjusted and Problem-Free Groups

| Test # or Name | Function | 1 | 2 | 3 | 5 |
|---|---|---|---|---|---|
| Frostig I | Fine motor control—simple | | .01 | .01 | .05 |
| Frostig II | Visual perc.—form discrimination | | .01 | | |
| Frostig III | Visual perc.—constancy | .01 | .01 | .05 | .01 |
| Frostig IV | Visual perc.—orientation in space | | .01 | .05 | .01 |
| Frostig V | Visual perc.—orientation in space | .01 | .05 | .01 | |
| Bender-Gestalt | Fine motor control—complex | .01 | .01 | .01 | .01 |
| Raven Matrices | Symbolic integ.—with concrete materials | .01 | .01 | .05 | .05 |
| ITPA-Vis. Decod. | Symbolic integration—nonverbal | .05 | | | |
| ITPA-Mot. Encod. | Linguistic input | | .01 | | |
| I-A | Visual perception—form | .01 | .05 | | |
| I-B | Visual perception—form, simple | | .01 | .01 | |
| I-D | Visual perception—form, complex | .05 | .05 | | |
| I-E | Visual perception—constancy | .01 | .01 | .01 | .01 |
| I-F | Visual perception—constancy | | .01 | .01 | .01 |
| II-A | Aud. perc.—discrim. of similarities & diffs. | .05 | .05 | .05 | .05 |
| II-B | Auditory perception—constancy | .01 | .01 | .01 | .01 |
| III-A | Visual memory—form | | .01 | | |
| III-B | Memory—immedate meaningful | | .05 | | .01 |
| III-C | Memory—immediate meaningful | .05 | | | |
| III-E | Memory—delayed meaningful | | .01 | | |
| IV-A | Orientation—time | .01 | .01 | .01 | .01 |
| IV-B | Orientation—size | .01 | .01 | .01 | |
| IV-C | Orientation—midline | | .01 | | |
| IV-D | Orientation—space | .01 | .01 | | .01 |
| IV-F | Orientation—space | .05 | | | |
| V-A | Integration—nonverbal | .01 | | .01 | |
| V-B | Symbolic integration | | .01 | .05 | |
| V-C | Symbolic integration—abstract | .01 | .01 | | |
| V-D | Symbolic integration—abstract | .01 | .01 | .01 | .01 |
| V-E | Symbolic integration—numerical | .01 | .01 | .01 | |
| VI-A | Fine motor control | .01 | .01 | .01 | .01 |
| VI-B | Eye-hand coordination | .01 | .01 | .01 | .05 |
| VII | Gross motor coordination—jumping | .01 | .05 | | .05 |
| VII | Identification—gross motor coord. | .01 | | .01 | |
| VIII-A | Linguistic input—total score | .01 | | .01 | |
| IX-D | Tactile kinesthetic—face-hand | | | .05 | |
| IX-E | Tactile kinesthetic—moving stimulus | .01 | | .01 | .01 |
| IX-F | Tactile kinesthetic—motor memory (left) | .05 | .05 | | |
| IX-F | Tactile kinesthetic—motor memory (right) | .01 | | | |
| IX-F | Tactile kinesthetic—motor memory (total) | .01 | | | |

block." Since many of the children who have deficits in CPM areas show consequent difficulty with coping and resultant secondary emotional problems, the manifestation of these symptoms in the school and the concentration by the clinic on measurement of inter-personal variables have often obscured the presence of the CPM def-icits.

In order to develop an appropriate battery of tests for identifica-tion of the CPM child, it was necessary to predict the skills that are crucial to school learning and general adjustment. The final list grew out of a search of the literature to determine which variables had in the past been found to relate to school problems and resulted from the experience of the members of the Lafayette Clinic group. The variables selected for measurement include: visual perception (discrimination and constancy); auditory perception (discrimination and constancy); fine motor control (simple and complex); tactile perception; gross motor coordination (eye-hand, extremities); ori-entation (space, size, time); linguistics (input, output); memory (im-mediate rote, immediate, meaningful, and delayed rote); integration (nonverbal and symbolic) (see table 1).

In the original study, the maladjusted and problem-free children were compared on a wide-scale battery of tests, including the Wechsler Intelligence Scale for Children. The CPM battery con-sisted of some standardized tests drawn from achievement test bat-teries and others that were designed for this study. Some of the stan-dardized tests were adapted for use in this study with the permission of the publishers. Forty of the test scores discriminated significantly between the two groups, some at all grade levels, some at only one or two. The total list is presented in table 9. The CPM dysfunction score (see chap. 2) was derived from this set of scores.

A refined battery of twenty tests was subsequently determined (see table 10), which retained the items that provided the highest correlations with the total dysfunction score derived from the full battery. This refined 20-test battery is probably the most effective and efficient instrument, for it contains representative items from each CPM area. Table 10 lists these tests and indicates the measures for each grade that can be used with adequate reliability. The corre-lation between the simplified battery and the refined battery for

## table 10

### Refined Test Battery and Simplified Battery for Each Grade

| Test Name | Grade 1 and 2 * | Grade 3 † | Grade 5 ‡ |
|---|---|---|---|
| Frostig III | A§ | | A |
| Frostig IV | C | K | |
| I-B | I | E | |
| I-E | | J | C |
| I-F | | H | |
| II-A | J | G | |
| II-B | G | C | F |
| III-A | | | I |
| III-E | E | | |
| IV-A | | | E |
| IV-B | | | |
| V-D | | B | |
| V-E | B | | |
| VI-A | H | | |
| VI-B | | F | G |
| VII | F | | D |
| VIII-A | | I | |
| IX-E | | | H |
| Raven | | A | J |
| Bender | D | D | B |

\* R = .797  † R = .972  ‡ R = .916

§ At each grade level, the tests are ordered by letter symbol according to the amount contributed to the total R. The simplified battery, then, consists of all lettered tests.

grades one and two is .797; for grade three, .972; and for grade five, .916. From this table, it is possible for practitioners with a limited amount of time to construct a simpler battery that correlates with the total 20 test battery. Using this method, CPM dysfunction can be determined, although not all areas of CPM functioning are measured.

The standardized tests used unchanged in the battery are available from the publishers. The average scores obtained by our problem-free sample are included in the normative tables which appear in appendix C and may be used to determine the CPM dysfunction score. Tests no longer available from the publishers, others for which we have permission to reproduce, and the new tests are to be found in appendix A. For these tests, the norms from this study are the only ones available.

## The Refined Battery of Tests

Thirty-one tests designed for this study plus nine standardized tests make up the total battery. The refined battery consists of twenty tests. These are discussed briefly here according to the type of tests and the CPM area measured and are listed in full in appendix A. Both grade and age norms are presented in appendix C.

### 1. Tests of Visual Perception

There are five tests in the total battery that measure varying aspects of visual perception. The emphasis is on perceptual discrimination and orientation in space. Two of the tests (I-E, I-F) are more complex, involving tachistoscopic presentation. The tests were derived from the Lee Clark Reading Readiness Test (Lee and Clark, 1960), Monroe Reading Aptitude Test (Monroe, 1935), and the Durrell Analysis of Reading Difficulty (Durrell, 1955). The tests from the battery are supplemented by tests 2, 3, 4, and 5 of the Frostig Developmental Test of Visual Perception. Tests I-B, I-E, and I-F are described in appendix A.

### 2. Tests of Auditory Perception

Tests II-A and II-B are used to measure auditory discrimination. Both were presented in this study using prerecorded tapes to eliminate visual cues and examiner differences. The discrimination test was devised by Irwin and Jensen (1963) for use with cerebral palsy children. The auditory constancy task was developed for this project. Both tests are described in appendix A.

### 3. Tests of Memory Function

The four memory tasks (III-A, B, C, and E) involve visual and auditory modes: nonverbal and verbal material with both immediate and delayed recall. The tests were derived from Monroe Reading Aptitude Test, Durrell Analysis of Reading Difficulty, and the Detroit Reading Readiness Test (1962). Tests III-A and III-E are contained in appendix A.

## 4. Tests of Orientation

The orientation tests covering time (IV-A), space (IV-D and IV-F), and size (IV-B) involve measurement of both concept and information. The time and size orientation tests were adapted from a questionnaire by Pollack and Goldfarb (1957); other size and space tests were derived from the New York Test of Arithmetical Meanings (Wrightstone et al., 1956) and the Lee Clark Reading Readiness Test. The test for midline orientation (IV-C), ability to cross over the midline of the body, was taken from Ayres (1966). Tests IV-A and IV-B are described in appendix A.

## 5. Tests of Integration

In this section both verbal symbolic and nonverbal conceptualization were measured. Simple jigsaw puzzles were used for nonverbal integration, supplemented by the Raven Progressive Matrices Test (Raven, 1960). The tests of verbal integration included subtests from the California Test of Mental Maturity (Sullivan et al., 1957), Monroe Reading Aptitude Tests, Gates Reading Test (Gates, 1958), Gates Reading Survey (Gates, 1942), and California Achievement Test (Tiegs and Clark, 1957). The last two were supplemented by original items to extend the range of difficulty. Included in appendix A are tests V-D and V-E.

## 6. Tests of Fine Motor Control

The tests used here involve perceptual-motor behavior but the scoring emphasis was on motor control. Two fine motor control tests were devised for this study and have been previously reported (Llorens and Rubin, 1967). Test 1 from the Frostig supplements those tests in this area. In addition, the Bender Visual Motor Gestalt Test, administered and scored according to Koppitz (1963), was used. Both tests VI-A and VI-B are included in appendix A.

## 7. Tests of Gross Motor Coordination

Of the several tests from the Kephart Perceptual Survey (Kephart, 1962) utilized, only jumping and identification of body parts were retained. Test VII, jumping and identification, is included in appendix A.

## 8. Linguistics Tests

Items from the Gates Basic Reading Test (Gates, 1958) were adopted for this section of the battery and comprise test VIII-A as part of the refined test (appendix A). This is a test of auditory decoding and was supplemented by two tests from the Illinois Test of Psycholinguistic Abilities: visual decoding and motor encoding.

## 9. Tests of Tactile and Kinesthetic Perception

For tactile discrimination, five tests were adopted for this battery. In all tests, visual cues were eliminated as the subject was asked to locate a single stimulus or two simultaneous stimuli on the hand, recognize a simple form drawn on the hand, or recognize simple geometric forms by touch. The Face-Hand Test reported by Pollack and Goldfarb (1957) was also used. The motor memory test from the Ayres 40-Test Battery (1966) and the Seguin Form Board, administered with vision occluded, were the items used for measures of kinesthetic perception. Test IX-E is included in the refined battery (appendix A).

## Summary

By utilizing a comprehensive battery of tests designed to measure functioning in nine different cognitive-perceptual-motor areas, it is possible to determine if a child is significantly below his age-mates in those skills required for learning. Moreover, upon determining significant CPM dysfunction, it is possible to hypothesize that a developmental disorder does play a major role in the child's maladjusted behavior. Such an interpretation, when supplemented by other data, can lead to a relevant remedial program. The interpretation of these test findings and the planning of remedial programs will be discussed in the following chapters.

# chapter four

# INTERPRETATION OF
# THE TEST RESULTS

We have demonstrated repeatedly that it is possible to train an intelligent, stable, mature, nonprofessional individual to administer the cognitive-perceptual-motor battery with reliable results, and we have also emphasized repeatedly that the job of interpreting the results must be the responsibility of the clinical psychologist or educational psychologist who is thoroughly trained in the psychopathology of children.

There is perhaps nothing more important to be stressed in the interpretation of the results of the CPM battery than that the interpretation must be done within the larger context of the child's intellectual and personality functioning. The CPM assessment is most significant in the context of a total psychological evaluation which includes an individual intelligence test and projective materials.

That there is a necessity for appropriate intelligence testing is shown by the enthusiasm for the discovery that deficits in certain areas will make classroom learning difficult for some children. This seems to have led some professional people—who obviously should know better—and some parents to forget that there is such a phenomenon as a mentally retarded child for whom retraining and remediation are *not* magic wands. There is some evidence that a retarded child might improve in his behavior and might acquire some additional reading or arithmetic skills if he receives the benefit of special techniques which are designed to take cognizance of his obvious CPM deficits. Nevertheless, it may be found that a retarded child at the end of such a training program might retain his long-term occupational or self-care limitations exactly as they were before. Discoveries that will compensate for mental retardation and change the individual's essential inability to adapt independently to his environment have not been made at this time. We do not advocate the use of the CPM battery by itself unless it is intended as an initial screening to be followed by other selected evaluation measures.

## Use of Abbreviated Scales

The size of the CPM battery frequently brings from school personnel protests that they do not have the time to give such a complete assessment to every child who is referred to them, especially in view of the necessity for intelligence and personality measures.

A composite battery can provide indications of CPM dysfunction in a child already referred because of maladjustment. A few of the tests may be used as a preliminary screening instrument to select those subjects who would receive the entire battery. It is possible, however, on the basis of only a few measures, to select the child with symptomatic problems secondary to CPM limitations, but planning for an individual child requires a more complete assessment (see chap. 3). The more complete battery is desirable to draw a profile which can prove a meaningful basis for remedial intervention.

## Interpreting the Profile

Comprehensive assessment of a wide variety of skills provides the schools with information that is useful for understanding the child's symptoms and for planning programs. It supplements the standard I.Q. and achievement tests with a delineation of strengths and weaknesses related to learning demands. It provides information from which it is possible to determine whether the child's symptoms are secondary to stress resulting from the interaction of CPM dysfunction and school expectations. It can give school social workers some directions to explore in their search for the role of the home in the total problem.

For each child, the CPM battery measures current functioning levels and compares them with the performances of other children of like age and grade. In this age of computers, it is popular to view the human animal as an information processing system and the evaluation battery enables the examiner to determine whether difficulties lie in input—perceptual processes, central integrative functions, such as reasoning and memory—or in output, including fine and gross motor coordination. By using the normative tables, the age level at which the child is functioning can be determined or, alternatively, the grade level (see appendix C). For the practitioner wishing to conceptualize the tests in terms of input, integration, and output, the following grouping of the tests might be useful and interesting:

| *Perceptual* | *Test* |
|---|---|
| Tactile Discrimination | IX-D and IX-E |
| Kinesthetic Discrimination | IX-F |
| Visual Form Discrimination | I-A and I-B |
| Visual Spatial Orientation | Frostig IV and I-D |
| Visual Form Constancy | Frostig III, I-E, and I-F |
| Auditory Discrimination | II-A |
| Auditory Constancy | II-B |
| Language Input | VIII-A |

| *Integrative Functions* | |
|---|---|
| Verbal Symbolic Reasoning | V-B, V-C, and V-E |
| Inferential Reasoning | V-D |
| Time Orientation | IV-A |
| Space Orientation | IV-C, IV-D, and IV-F |
| Size Orientation | IV-B |
| Auditory Memory Immediate Recall | III-B and III-C |
| Visual Memory Immediate Recall | III-A |
| Auditory Memory Delayed Recall | III-E |
| Nonverbal Integration | V-A and Raven Progressive Matrices Percentile Score |

*Motor Output*

| Fine Motor Control | VI-A, VI-B, and Bender-Gestalt |
|---|---|
| Gross Motor Coordination | Jumping and Identification, Kephart Tests |

Each child's strengths and weaknesses can be graphically represented. In this way uneven functioning, if present, can be dramatically displayed. Some examples drawn from the Roseville study are presented, incorporating information from the classroom, utilizing the CPM battery to outline a remedial plan. In the preparation of these profiles, grade norms were used. When a score fell within plus or minus one standard deviation for the total grade, it was judged to be average; a score at plus one standard deviation or above was judged above average; a score at minus one standard deviation was judged below average; and any score below minus two standard deviations was called very poor. Only the scores from the refined battery were utilized: those tests which discriminated between experimental and control groups at any grade level.

## Clinical Examples

Case Example no. 1

Barry was nine years and five months old when he was identified by the third grade teacher as maladjusted. On the basis of high scores on the Behavior Checklist he was included in our experimental sample. Those items which were checked three times, indicating they were shown frequently, are:

6. Aggressive in underhanded ways
7. Seeks attention excessively
8. Very short attention span
10. Shows signs of nervousness (nailbiting, crying, tics, rocking)
17. Lacks responsibility for self, always has excuse for shortcomings
18. Resists limits or rules in group games
26. Makes odd noises

29. Is disoriented in space, is confused as to directions given
31. Tendencies toward primitive hostilities, temper tantrums, wild destruction
33. Antisocial tendencies (steals, lies, destroys property, bullies, defies, resents discipline)

In the second grade, Barry was about a half year retarded in reading and arithmetic but by the time he was in the fourth grade he was about two and a half years retarded in these subjects.

On the standard test of intelligence, the Wechsler Intelligence Scale for Children, he was found to be functioning within the average range with a verbal I.Q. of 96, a performance I.Q. of 107, and a full scale I.Q. of 101. There was considerable variation on the verbal scale with scores ranging from 6 (digit span) to 11 (similarities). Scores on the nonverbal scale were more uniform with only the block design subtest below 10. He obtained a scale score of 15 on object assembly and picture completion. The Frostig tests revealed below-age functioning on four of the five subtests with scores as low as 5 (Test III, form constancy) and 6 (Test I, eye-motor coordination). The Raven Progressive Matrices Percentile Score was 18, within the range of average functioning for our group of third graders.

His performance on the Lafayette Clinic CPM battery shows marked intra-individual variation with many scores at a level of minus one standard deviation and some below minus two standard deviations, when compared to grade norms (see table 11). The pattern of these scores, shown in figure 2, provides a graphic demonstration of areas of strengths and weaknesses. The profile of scores indicates special weakness in the integrative functions including abstract reasoning, spatial concepts, and memory functioning, involving both visual and auditory modalities. In addition to these areas of dysfunction he shows weakness in fine and gross motor coordination. The overall dysfunction score was 10, well within the range of the maladjusted sample.

This information, derived from the CPM battery, indicates high intra-individual variable functioning of this child only hinted at by the verbal-performance I.Q. discrepancy and the variability noted within the Wechsler Intelligence Scale for Children verbal scale.

# table II

## Lafayette Clinic CPM Battery Summary Score Sheet

NAME    BARRY         GRADE    3    AGE    9 yrs. 5 mos.

-------------------------------------------------------------------

### SERIES I
*Visual Perception*

| | |
|---|---|
| A | 13 |
| B | 22 |
| D | 8 |
| E | 13 |
| F | 51.5 |

### SERIES II
*Auditory Perception*

| | |
|---|---|
| A | 21 |
| B | 19 |

### SERIES III
*Memory*

| | |
|---|---|
| A | 13.5 |
| B | 6 |
| C | 19 |
| E | 6 |

### SERIES IV
*Orientation*

| | |
|---|---|
| A | 22 |
| B | 16 |
| C | 0 |
| D | 12 |
| F | 5 |

### SERIES V
*Integration*

| | |
|---|---|
| A | 401 sec. |
| B | 12 |
| C | 29 |
| D | 12 |
| E | 11 |

### SERIES VI
*Fine Motor Control*

| | |
|---|---|
| Total A | 7 |
| Total B | 2 |

### SERIES VII
*Gross Motor Coordination*

| | | |
|---|---|---|
| 4 | Jumping | 5 |
| 5 | Ident. | 8 |

### SERIES VIII
*Linguistics-Input*

| | |
|---|---|
| A | 14 |

### SERIES IX
*Tactile and Kinesthetic*

| | |
|---|---|
| D | 10 |
| E | 4 |
| F - Left | 20.5 |
| F - Right | 17.0 |
| F - Total | 37.5 |

BENDER KOPPITZ SCORE:    6

RAVEN PERCENTILE:    18%

### *Frostig*

| | |
|---|---|
| 1 | 6 |
| 2 | 10 |
| 3 | 5 |
| 4 | 7 |
| 5 | 7 |

52

INDIVIDUAL PROFILE

Name  BARRY                                                    Age  9 yrs. 5 mos.

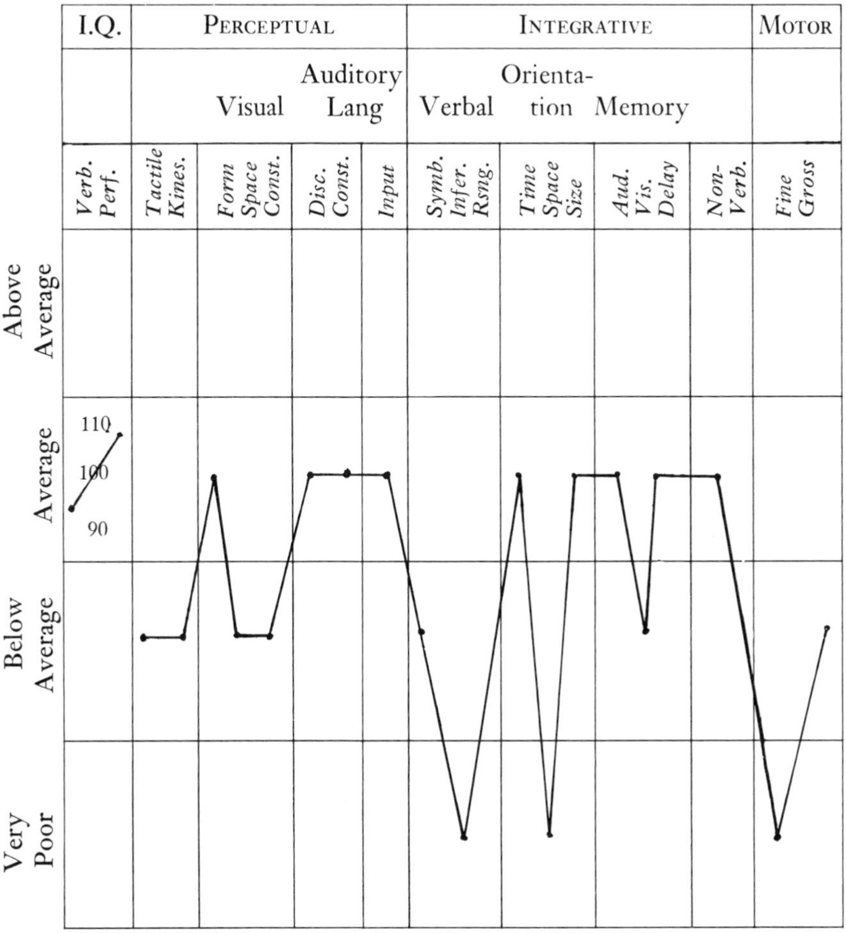

*Figure 2. CPM Profile*—BARRY

Based on our clinical research we expect such a youngster to approach the learning tasks with significant limitations affecting progress in learning. With some limitation in visual perception, coupled with memory and fine motor control dysfunction, learning to read and the carry over of learning in the early grades would be especially difficult. With evidence pointing to dysfunction in abstract reasoning, one would anticipate further problems in the fourth grade and later where there is more reliance on comprehension skills. His most recent achievement test scores, showing two and a half years' retardation in the middle of the fourth grade, confirmed this prediction. The report from the principal at the end of the year indicated that he would be failed.

Barry experiences considerable stress in school and probably has from the very beginning. His poor coordination, both fine and gross, has probably contributed also to feelings of inadequacy in his attempts to compete with the other boys. His reaction, according to the symptoms displayed in school, appears to be an aggressive, hostile one. By the third grade, the symptoms of disorientation are less noticeable to the teacher than his hostile behavior. We would hypothesize that much of his behavior maladjustment is secondary to the stress and anxiety he experiences in attempting to compete with others in play and in school.

Barry was included in our special skill training program. An individualized program of skill training was determined for him from his test scores, emphasizing first the perceptual and motor areas and then the verbal abstract functions.

## Case Example no. 2

The maladjusted behavior displayed by Danny when he was identified by his second grade teacher was somewhat different from the first case. According to his initial Behavior Checklist, the items checked three times were:

   8. Very short attention span
   9. Can't work independently
  27. Makes irrelevant or inappropriate remarks
  28. Misinterprets simple statements

In addition, the following items were checked two times:

  12. Daydreams
  15. Poor coordination (trouble with buttoning, tying shoes, getting shoes on correct feet)
  29. Is disoriented in space, is confused as to directions given

This complex of symptoms suggests a somewhat immature youngster, inattentive and aloof with definite evidences of disorientation to his environment. He was included in our experimental sample of maladjusted children and received the complete testing. In addition, he was the subject for a sub-study in which he received a neurological examination, EEG, psychiatric examination, and full developmental and social history data was obtained from the mother. At the time of testing, Danny was approximately six months retarded in reading, three months advanced in arithmetic, and about six months retarded on the overall Metropolitan Achievement Test.

On the Wechsler Intelligence Scale for Children, Danny received an overall full scale I.Q. of 100, showing more capabilities on the verbal scale (verbal I.Q. 108) than on the performance test (performance I.Q. 92).

The range of functioning on the verbal scale was from a scale score of 9 on vocabulary to a scale score of 17 on similarities. Conceptual thinking seemed quite advanced. On the nonverbal scale, two of the tests were definitely below average. On picture arrangement and object assembly he obtained scale scores of 7 and his highest score was on picture completion, a score of 11. All of his test scores on the Frostig Test were age appropriate, his Koppitz Bender Score was 3, well below the average for our second grade sample, and his Raven Percentile Score of 85 indicated well above average functioning in the nonverbal integration areas.

On the CPM battery, Danny showed a total dysfunction score of 6 which is the lowest limit for the high dysfunction group. All of his scores from the refined battery are presented in table 12, from which the profile shown in figure 3 was drawn.

Although Danny's profile does not show dips into the very poor category, it is apparent that there is marked intra-individual variability among the various cognitive, perceptual, and motor skills. Verbal symbolic functions, visual and auditory discrimination functions appear to be adequate but memory functioning is certainly disturbed, whether visual or auditory modalities are utilized. Fine and gross motor coordination are definitely below average along with kinesthetic perception. Orientation for time and size is also low in this

## table 12
### *Lafayette Clinic CPM Battery Summary Score Sheet*

NAME      DANNY      GRADE    2    AGE     8 yrs. 3 mos.

-----------------------------------------------------------------

### SERIES I
### *Visual Perception*

| | |
|---|---|
| A | 20 |
| B | 18 |
| D | 8 |
| E | 7 |
| F | 34.5 |

### SERIES II
### *Auditory Perception*

| | |
|---|---|
| A | 22 |
| B | 16 |

### SERIES III
### *Memory*

| | |
|---|---|
| A | 14.0 |
| B | 13 |
| C | 25 |
| E | 7 |

### SERIES IV
### *Orientation*

| | |
|---|---|
| A | 15 |
| B | 15 |
| C | 6 |
| D | 15 |
| F | 8 |

### SERIES V
### *Integration*

| | |
|---|---|
| A | 300 sec. |
| B | 10 |
| C | 21 |
| D | 16 |
| E | 11 |

### SERIES VI
### *Fine Motor Control*

| | |
|---|---|
| Total A | 7 |
| Total B | 2 |

### SERIES VII
### *Gross Motor Coordination*

| | | |
|---|---|---|
| 4 | Jumping | 6 |
| 5 | Ident. | 5 |

### SERIES VIII
### *Linguistics-Input*

| | |
|---|---|
| A | 14 |

### SERIES IX
### *Tactile and Kinesthetic*

| | | |
|---|---|---|
| D | | 10 |
| E | | 7 |
| F | - Left | 32.5 |
| F | - Right | 24.0 |
| F | - Total | 56.5 |

BENDER KOPPITZ SCORE:    3

RAVEN PERCENTILE:    85%

### *Frostig*

| | |
|---|---|
| 1 | 10 |
| 2 | 8 |
| 3 | 9 |
| 4 | 10 |
| 5 | 10 |

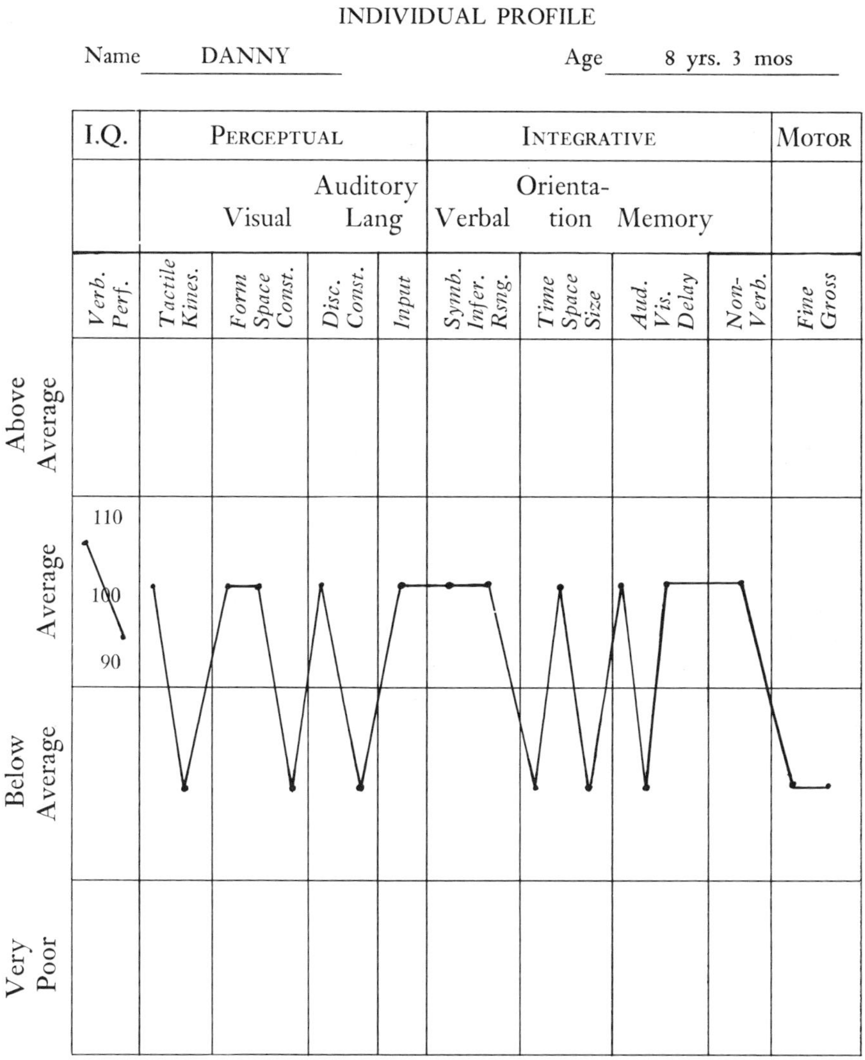
INDIVIDUAL PROFILE
Name DANNY
Age 8 yrs. 3 mos
I.Q.
PERCEPTUAL
INTEGRATIVE
MOTOR
Visual
Auditory Lang
Verbal
Orienta- tion
Memory
Verb. Perf.
Tactile Kines.
Form Space Const.
Disc. Const.
Input
Symb. Infer. Rsng.
Time Space Size
Aud. Vis. Delay
Non- Verb.
Fine Gross
Above Average
Average
Below Average
Very Poor
110
100
90

*Figure 3. CPM Profile-Danny*

profile. Even though there is a noticeable discrepancy between verbal and performance I.Q.s, both are within the average range and do not indicate, as does the CPM battery, the degree of variability to this boy's functioning. In contrast to the previous example, one would anticipate that Danny's problems would be most apparent in the primary grades where skills involving fine motor control and memory, especially visual memory functioning, are relied upon heavily. His good verbal skills should allow for continued progress in learning, although the presence of such marked variability would indicate continued difficulty in adjustment. When Danny was re-tested in the third grade for achievement, he was retarded slightly over one year in both reading and arithmetic. When he was entered into the special class for skill training, an individual program was prepared emphasizing primarily the perceptual-motor areas.

The additional clinical diagnostic information available on Danny is typical of the youngsters described by us as having high CPM dysfunction or by others as showing learning disability. There were positive findings only on the psychiatric interview, where he was described as a restless, jerky, somewhat immature youngster who was impulsive, distractible, and quick to give up in the face of frustration. He did not appear to be overly anxious, according to the psychiatrist, nor did he demonstrate unusual fears, hostility, or untoward perceptions of friends or parents or teachers. On both the neurological examination and the EEG, the findings were within normal limits. Facts from the social history indicated a youngster, first in the family, born at term, weighing between five and six pounds, following essentially an uneventful pregnancy on the part of the mother. He accomplished the milestones of development at the expected times and with the exception of some difficulties in toilet training was described as a responsive youngster, neither too active nor too quiet. There are certain factors, however, that are worthy of note. Mother is reported to have had a fall during the last trimester of her pregnancy with Danny and at the time of the delivery the child was held back. He was described as well and healthy at birth. When he began talking in sentences at nineteen to twenty-four months, his speech was initially unclear but improved subsequently. He was described as having adequate motor coordination as a preschooler and enjoyed both indoor and outdoor play. It is of some significance that his father who did not go beyond the eighth grade was described as having major problems similar to Danny's including both academic and behavior difficulties and, in addition, as having a history of behavior problems. There is also a history of epilepsy in the father's sister.

In general, these findings do not contribute to any definite neurological diagnosis to help explain Danny's poor adjustment in learning and behavior, but they do contribute mildly to the hypothesis that his development was in some way atypical, possibly related to genetic factors.

## Use of the Profile in the School

The special education teacher or remedial specialist is probably best equipped to utilize the CPM profile for individualized programming. By knowing the extent of the weaknesses and in what skills they lie, along with information from achievement tests, the specialist teacher can decide whether the child needs complete skill training in a specialized program or whether there are some areas that can be trained by the itinerant specialist, while the child continues in his regular grade. Information from the profile can be helpful to regular class teachers as well. Knowing that a child has special weaknesses in fine motor control and eye-hand coordination, for example, in the presence of other average or above average skills, may help her to be more understanding of the child's special difficulties with written work. These may be manifested by poor achievement, by slow or delayed productions, or by behavior difficulties, including lowered motivation. The school psychologist or teacher specialist can use this approach meaningfully to supply the classroom teacher with a better appreciation of individual differences.

## Use of the Profile with Parents

Performance at school is very often interpreted to parents as dependent on either I.Q. or emotional factors. We have demonstrated, by using the approach suggested in this study, how limitations in skill affect the child's achievement at different grades and with different subject materials. This interaction effect may be a crucial factor in understanding the child's motivational pattern. Administrators and school social workers can utilize the profile when appropriate to indicate the child's variable capacities and point out his areas of vulnerability. By this method it is often possible to generalize these findings to the home situation. In this manner, the parents can be helped to examine the child's behavior difficulties at home, recognizing what situations may put the child under stress in that setting. Continued counseling, either individually or with groups of parents, may contribute to a relief of stress for the child at home.

## Use of the Profile at the Mental Health Clinic

Just as the CPM child with secondary emotional disturbance cannot be distinguished on the basis of his behavior from the child with primary emotional disturbance in the classroom, he cannot be distinguished from children with psychiatric problems at the mental health clinic, unless he receives an evaluation of strengths and weaknesses including an assessment of developmental unevenness. The number of CPM children who are seen in a mental health clinic probably depends a great deal on the population from which the clinic is drawing and the sophistication of the school psychologist or other professional who might see the child before he reaches a clinic. At Lafayette Clinic, about 55 percent of the referrals to the Children's Service come from public schools and one review (April 1968) of just the inpatient children (ages six to twelve) showed that 81 percent of the twenty-two patients admitted to the hospital since July 1967 had severe CPM deficits. Eighteen of the twenty-two performed one or more standard deviations below the average for their age group on six or more tests. Fifty percent of this poor group demonstrated ten or more tests below this criterion. In the public school sample (Roseville) only twenty-four of 398 or 6 percent had a dysfunction score of 10 or more.

Since understanding of emotional disturbance is not complete without an assessment of stress factors operating at home and at school, an adequate social and developmental history and history of school performance are required. In some instances, the discovery of positive factors in the prenatal, birth, or developmental history helps to explain the source of the uneven development noted in the testing. In many cases, however, such facts are not uncovered. The reactions of the parents to some of the child's earlier inadequacies or the finding of traumatic situations in the family may help to explain the severity of the child's emotionally disturbed behavior.

Disposition of a child case in a mental health setting is an extremely complex matter. The child whose reactions are maladaptive may need psychotherapy in order to accept himself and to learn better ways of handling his anxiety, but, if there is no relief of stress in the environment, he may be unable to profit from psychotherapy. For many children a combined treatment program is essential— individual psychotherapy, counseling of the parents, and a retraining and remedial plan. For an intelligent selection of the treatment of choice, a comprehensive psychological evaluation of the child, including the CPM battery, is imperative.

## Other Uses of Profile

These profiles may be used for each individual to assess his skills and determine to what degree CPM dysfunction is a significant problem. The tests may be used at the early or later elementary level to screen groups of maladjusted children to identify those with higher dysfunction for whom remedial programs may be planned. The CPM battery may be used as a screening instrument at the kindergarten level to identify high-risk children for whom altered kindergarten and primary curricula may be introduced as part of a prevention program (Rubin, 1969).

# chapter five

# FROM EVALUATION TO TREATMENT

Treatment for the CPM child follows from the comprehensive assessment: remediation of deficit skill functioning; relief of stress in school; relief of stress from the family and increase of support within the family.

We begin with the assumption that intervention must be directed toward the immediate causative factors, avoiding the dilemma of traditional therapies that are derived from a diagnostic framework that searches for ultimate etiology. For many types of disturbances, uncovering the earlier antecedents of the present conflicts is an essential ingredient of the therapy. Since we do not know the primary causes of CPM dysfunction at this time, our treatment efforts must be directed toward minimizing the debilitating effects of this condition and restoring functioning, whenever possible, to a normal level. Our research findings have led to the view that many behavior disturbances in the classroom are secondary to significant developmental inadequacies. These are known to be capable of setting into motion a distorting interaction between child and environment and bringing about a negative impact on personality development which increases as the child gets older. Although this impact begins early in the child's life, as environmental demands are increased, the effects of this increase are recognized later as maladjusted behavior. For many children, this impact is at its peak when they enter school.

Treatment for the CPM child can begin early—in the preschool years—if the condition is recognized and diagnosed. With such early intervention, the debilitating effects of maturational slowness on emotional and personality development can be avoided or kept to a minimum. Such early secondary prevention programs we discuss in chapter 6.

The CPM child is more often discovered during the primary grades at school and intervention may be instituted at this time with excellent results. Our focus here is on this group. Beyond the primary grade years, the effectiveness of these methods is reduced. However, recognition of the problem with adequate comprehensive assessment can lead to intervention that may bring about better restoration of functioning than traditional psychotherapeutic methods alone.

## Research Background

The treatment methods were derived in part from the results of a research program that was designed to evaluate in a group of primary grade maladjusted children the effectiveness of a program of skill retraining on CPM dysfunction, on school and home adjustment. Testing out a particular remedial method was a follow-up to the first phase of our research which laid the groundwork for identification and description of the CPM child (see chapter 1).

Fifty-eight children were selected as subjects for this study. They were drawn from the ones identified in the first phase of our study as evidencing behavior maladjustment, CPM dysfunction, and learning disorder. These subjects were selected from the first, second, and third grades and assigned to three "treatment" groups to achieve equivalence in age, sex, mean I.Q., and mean CPM dysfunction scores (see table 13). In addition, all fifty-eight children scored at or above a CPM dysfunction score of 6, within the range of significant dysfunction as defined by the earlier study. All of the children were academically retarded, achieving a half grade or more below grade placement. All of the children were alike on significant dimensions that had been described previously on the Behavior Checklist by such terms as "sensitive to criticism, overconforming, aggressive, attention-seeking, dependent, poorly coordinated, lacking a sense of responsibility, isolated from others, preoccupied, frequently tardy, and easily fatigued."

## table 13
*Distribution of Sex, Age, I.Q., and Mean
Dysfunction Scores for Study Sample*

|  | Total | M | F | Mean Age (months) | Mean WISC IQ Score Verb. | Perf. | Full Scale | Mean Dysfunction Score |
|---|---|---|---|---|---|---|---|---|
| Group I | 30 | 22 | 8 | 106.8 | 95.1 | 97.8 | 96.0 | 8.4 |
| Group II | 14 | 10 | 4 | 106.5 | 93.1 | 98.9 | 95.4 | 7.9 |
| Group III | 14 | 10 | 4 | 111.4 | 91.1 | 95.6 | 92.6 | 7.6 |

Our attention was focused on the thirty children in the experimental or retraining group (Group I) who were seen in small classes of seven or eight with a certified teacher and teacher aide assigned to each group. CPM profiles were drawn for each child and functional areas for retraining were delineated to be used by the teacher in program planning. Children were removed from their regular class activities for half of each day of one semester, and were seen in a special physical facility rented for this purpose. For each two-hour daily session, two broad functional areas were concentrated on. In the perceptual and motor development room, specific exercises were devoted to improving tactile-kinesthetic perception, orientation in space and size, and nonverbal integration. In the cognitive and perceptual development room, there were materials and programs designed to improve auditory perception, memory, orientation in time, linguistics, symbolic integration, and inferential reasoning. A schematic presentation of the training techniques associated with each functional area is provided in table 14.

The remedial group (Group II), which served as one of our comparison groups, was also involved in the special facility half days, five days a week for a semester, and was organized, into two small groups of seven, each under the direction of a special education teacher and a teacher aide. Lesson plans were developed for the children in the remedial group based on their performance on achievement tests so that remediation could be provided in academic areas in which they were deficient, utilizing their areas of competence.

# table 14
## CPM Training Techniques

| FUNCTION | TRAINING TECHNIQUES |
|---|---|
| 1. Tactile-kinesthetic proprioceptive perception | Tactile-kinesthetic proprioceptive sequence which includes cutaneous stimulation, passive and resistive exercise; Identification of body parts, etc.; Identification of objects by touch with sight occluded; Assembling simple puzzles with sight occluded; Sandplay |
| 2. Gross motor coordination<br>a. Eye-hand | Eye exercises; Frostig worksheets; Visual motor worksheets; Follow the dot worksheets; Copying worksheets; Visual motor worksheets; Cutting out objects from magazines, etc.; Supp: Jacks, ringtoss, pegboard, sewing cards |
| b. Extremities | Bouncing a ball, beachball, two hands, dominant hand. Basketball, two hands, dominant hand. Tennis ball, dominant hand; Catching, Throwing, Batting; Walk on a line; Walk on a beam; Trampoline, Jumprope; Kicking; Hopping; Skipping |
| 3. Orientation<br>a. Space | Physical exercises: Rolling over; Crawling; Walk on a line; Walk on balance board; Identifying body parts using neuromuscular facilitation techniques; Human figure puzzles; Frostig worksheets; Drill in left-right using visual discrimination worksheets. Supp: Magnet board; Hokey Pokey; Simon Says |
| b. Size | Frostig worksheets. Supp: Magnet bd. |
| c. Time | Holiday & seasons worksheets; Time worksheets; Supp: Play clock; Play calendar; Tell time lotto; records |
| 4. Fine Motor Control | Tracing beginning with geometric form stencils, geometric patterns, through animal form patterns; Visual motor worksheets; Tracing worksheets; Coloring worksheets |
| 5. Visual Perception<br>a. Discrimination | Flash cards (objects, letters, numbers, words); Visual discrimination worksheets; Frostig worksheets. Supp: Magnet board |
| b. Constancy | Frostig worksheets; Visual discrimination worksheets for similarities covering up stimulus object |
| 6. Auditory Perc.<br>a. Discrimination | Listening exercises; Rhythm band & objects; Sound cylinders; Rhyming worksheets; Initial consonant worksheets. Supp Games |
| b. Constancy | Rhyming worksheets; Initial consonant worksheets |
| 7. Linguistics Input | Direction records; Oral commands; Written commands |
| 8. Memory<br>a. Immediate rote | Visual: Flash cards—objects, letters, numbers, words, phrases<br>Auditory: Naming objects, letters, numbers and words |
| b. Immediate meaningful | Nursery rhymes; Sentences; Poems; Paragraphs; Stories and events |
| c. Delayed | Same as for immediate but with a time lapse |
| 9. Integration<br>a. Non-verbal | Graded puzzles; Frostig worksheets; Visual discrimination worksheets; Visual motor worksheets |
| b. Symbolic | Useful language worksheets; categorization puzzles; thinking skills worksheets; independent activities worksheets; Supp: Who gets it game; Lotto games; Play store game; Match & check; Play horse game. Numerical: Blocks & objects; Number readiness worksheets; Arithmetic readiness workbooks. Supp: Number readiness games |
| c. Integration Infer. Rsng. | Reading thinking skills worksheets |
| 10. Linguistics Output | SeeQuees puzzles; Picture scrapbook; Supplying endings; Telling stories and events |

## table 15
### *Distribution of Subjects by Grade and Group* *

Number of Subjects

| Grade | Group I | Group II | Group III | Totals |
|---|---|---|---|---|
| 1 | 9 | 6 | 8 | 23 |
| 2 | 12 | 6 | 1 | 19 |
| 3 | 9 | 2 | 5 | 16 |
| TOTALS | 30 | 14 | 14 | 58 |

* Differences in grade level representation are taken into account in the statistical analysis.

The final group of subjects, who comprised our "no treatment" controls (Group III), remained in the regular classroom in the public schools with one certified teacher in each classroom. Class sizes for the Roseville Schools range from twenty-six to thirty-three children per classroom, the modal class size being thirty.

The distribution of subjects by grade for each group is provided in table 15.

### The Stimulation Retraining Method

In this study, the emphasis was on the retraining method. There were no special attempts to reduce stress in the regular classroom concurrent with the special procedure. No specific program for the regular classroom teachers was carried out. The teachers were informed generally of the goals of the special class program, but no interpretations of the individual children's problems were given, nor was there any advice offered regarding special handling techniques. The parents, too, were informed of the program, obtaining their permission for inclusion of their child, but were not offered any individualized counseling or interpretation of their child's problems. The general nature of CPM dysfunction and the methods considered valuable which would be used in retraining were discussed with small groups of parents.

At the beginning of the program, soon after the start of the spring semester, the teachers were asked to fill out a Teacher's Rat-

## table 16
## *Teachers Rating Scale*
## *Sample Scale*

*Quarrelsomeness*

1. Child very seldom gets involved in disputes, quarrels, or fights with other children.
3.
5. Child quarrels and fights with other children about as much as is expected at his age.
7.
9. Child's contact with others very often results in arguments, quarreling, fighting, etc. (regardless of who started it).

ing Scale (see table 16) on all the children included in the study. In a previous study (Rubin, Simson & Betwee, 1966) this scale had demonstrated its usefulness as an instrument to measure classroom adjustment. In addition, achievement test scores were obtained from the records of all children previously tested or from new tests given to those not previously examined. The Metropolitan Achievement Test was utilized. Finally, a trained interviewer visited the home of each child and, on the basis of an interview with the mother, completed the Home Adjustment Scale (see table 17). Examples of the items from these two scales are given in tables 16 and 17. A fuller description of these instruments is provided in the final research report, "An Investigation of an Evaluation Method and Retraining Procedures for Emotionally Handicapped Children with Cognitive-Motor Deficits," which is available through Educational Research Information Center.

## table 17
## *Home Adjustment Scale*
## *Sample Scale*

*Attitude Toward School* (Items #1 and #2)

1. Likes to go, expresses interest and willingness, brings home materials proudly, comments favorably about the experience. Shows no resistance to school.
2. Talks resistance but goes regularly.
3. Plays sick, looks for excuses to miss school.
4. Generally unfavorable attitude, expresses dissatisfactions openly, or doesn't talk about school, frequently resistant or makes attempts to avoid school. Needs considerable urging to get going.

The semester was the full period during which this experiment took place; at its end the same instruments were repeated on all subjects in all three groups. In addition, the CPM battery was repeated. Test-retest comparisons between the three groups of children thus formed the basis for our conclusions regarding the effectiveness of the CPM training method with a sample of school maladjusted children.

## The Concept of Intervention

Cognitive-perceptual-motor retraining refers to techniques which are geared to the development of functional skills in children where such functioning has not taken place naturally. Furthermore, such deficit functioning is frequently a major factor in academic failure and behavior maladjustment. Repetition and reinforcement of appropriate behaviors form the basis for all training techniques. Beginning at the level within a given skill where a child achieves immediate success, opportunity is provided for practice with materials and objects. These materials increase in complexity and are presented in a graded sequence as the child shows mastery. The activities utilized in CPM training consist of educational games, readiness materials, physical rehabilitative treatment techniques, and specifically designed programs. A suggested list of useful materials for training each functional area appears in the accompanying table (see table 18). The works of Ayres (1963), Cruickshank (1961), DeHirsh (1966), Delacato (1959), and Doman (1960), Frostig (1968), Barsch (1962), and Bateman (1964) are similar both conceptually and methodologically to the programs promoted here. All of these programs are based upon the concept of a developmental continuum with the objective of initiating training as early in the developmental scale as needed for those skills that are demonstrated to be deficit. This is in contrast to other remedial methods which rely heavily on the substitution of compensatory modes of adaptation.

In addition to stimulation of deficit skills, other keys to successful programming include application of training to a range of skills, developmental sequencing, and overlearning. Initially, many workers in the field focused on one or two major functions and pre-

68

table 18

*Cognitive-Perceptual-Motor Functions, Definitions, Assessment Techniques and Suggested Training Techniques*

| FUNCTION | DEFINITION | ASSESSMENT TECHNIQUES | TRAINING TECHNIQUES |
|---|---|---|---|
| 1. Tactile-Kinesthetic Proprioceptive Perception | Central Response to stimuli presented only to tactual senses—inferred from behavior response | Lafayette Clinic Tactile-Kinesthetic-Proprioceptive Perception Test | Tactile-Kinesthetic Proprioceptive sequence which includes cutaneous stimulation, passive and resistive exercise<br>Identification of body parts, etc.<br>Identification of objects by touch with sight occluded<br>Assembling simple puzzles with sight occluded<br>Sand Play |
| 2. Gross Motor Coordination | Coordination of large muscles in purposeful manner, including eyehand coordination and coordination of extremities | | |
| a. Eye-hand | Ability to use muscles to perform coordinated tasks such as cutting | Frostig Development Test of Visual Perception I | Eye-Exercises<br>Frostig worksheets<br>Visual Motor worksheets<br>Follow the Dot worksheets<br>Copying worksheets<br>Visual Motor worksheets<br>Cutting out objects from magazines, etc.<br>Supp: Jacks, ringtoss, pegboard, sewing cards |
| b. Extremities | Smooth functioning of arms and legs, as in walking | Kephart Perceptual Survey | Bouncing a ball, beachball, two hands dominant hand. Basketball, two hands dominant hand. Tennis ball, dominant hand |

table 18 (*Continued*)

| FUNCTION | DEFINITION | ASSESSMENT TECHNIQUES | TRAINING TECHNIQUES |
|---|---|---|---|
| Gross Motor Coordination (continued) | | | Catching<br>Roll ball to child sitting on the floor<br>Have child bounce a balloon in the air, keeping it aloft<br>Throw balloon to child, keep aloft between you<br>Beach ball<br>Volley ball<br>Soft ball<br>Throwing a ball<br>Throwing a ball in a:<br>  Wastebasket<br>  Horseshoes<br>  Ringtoss<br>  Bean bag throw<br>  Dart throw<br>  Shooting baskets<br>Throwing a ball at a wall target<br>Batting a ball<br>Hit ball on a stationary string with a paddle<br>Hit ball on a stationary string with a bat<br>Hit ball on a moving string with a paddle<br>Hit ball on a moving string with a bat<br>Throw ball to child at short distance, let child use paddle. After success use bat.<br>  Increase distance<br>Walk on a line<br>Walking beam<br>Trampoline |

| | | | |
|---|---|---|---|
| Gross Motor Coordination (continued) | | | Jumping rope, simple & complex<br>Kick ball from a stationary position<br>(Soccer ball to volleyball)<br>Kick ball while being rolled to him<br>Kick football held in own hands |
| 3. Orientation | Awareness of relationships between the child and events and objects in the environment, along the dimensions of time, space, and size | | |
| a. Space | | Frostig Test III and V; New York Test of Arithmetical Meanings<br>Level I, Test I (7, 8, 12, 13, 26–32)<br>Level II, Test I (2, 3, 6, 7)<br>Lee Clark Test III (11, 14, 19)<br>Lafayette Clinic Questionnaire | Physical Exercises<br>Rolling over<br>Crawling<br>Walk on a line<br>Walk on balance board<br>Identifying body parts using neuromuscular facilitation techniques<br>Human figure puzzles<br>Frostig worksheets<br>Drill in left-right using visual discrimination worksheets<br>Supp:<br>Magnet board<br>Hokey pokey<br>Simon says |
| b. Size | | Orientation Question-NYTA Level I, Test I (1–4, 14–17, 22–25)<br>Level II, Test II (1, 9)<br>Lee Clark Test III (9, 10, 12) | Frostig worksheets<br><br>Supp: Magnet board |

table 18 (*Continued*)

| FUNCTION | DEFINITION | ASSESSMENT TECHNIQUES | TRAINING TECHNIQUES |
|---|---|---|---|
| 4. Fine Motor Control | Control of fine motor movements in simple and complex situations | Frosting Test I<br>Bender-Gestalt<br>L-R Fine Motor Control Test | Tracing beginning with geometric form stencils, geometric patterns, through animal form patterns<br>Visual Motor worksheets<br>Tracing worksheets<br>Coloring worksheets |
| 5. Visual Perception | Central response to visual stimulus, inferred from verbal or motor response | | |
| a. Discrimination | Recognition of similarities and differences when the stimuli are increasingly similar checked along various visual dimensions, including form, size, and space | Form: Lee Clark, Test I (S)<br>Test IV   Frosting<br>Space: Monroe Reading Aptitude, Vis. Test I | Flash cards<br>  (objects, letters, numbers, words)<br>Visual Discrimination worksheets<br>Frostig worksheets<br>Supp: Magnet board |
| b. Constancy | Holding of a symbolic representation of a form, in both simple and complex stimulus situations | Frostig Test IV<br>Durrell Vis. Memory of Words<br>Durrell Vis. Memory of Letters<br>  (Beginning and Intermediate) | Frostig worksheets<br>Visual Discrimination worksheets for similarities covering up stimulus objects |
| 6. Auditory Perception | Central response to auditory stimulus | | |
| a. Discrimination | Recognition of similarity and difference between auditorily presented stimuli, not musical sounds but rather language symbols | Sound Discrimination Test<br>Wepman Test | Listening exercises<br>Sound objects<br>Tape recorded worksheets<br>Paired word lists<br>Rhyming worksheets<br>Phonics worksheets<br>Supp: Games |

| | | | |
|---|---|---|---|
| b. Constancy | Hold a memory of an auditory stimulus and recognize it among competing stimuli | Lafayette Clinic Test of Auditory Constancy | Phonics worksheets<br>Supp:<br>Play clock<br>Tell time<br>Lotto |
| 7. Orientation Time | (See Item #3) | Lafayette Clinic Orientation Questionnaire | Problems in before, after, now, later<br>Season coloring sheets<br>Time worksheets<br>Play calendar<br>Supp:<br>Play clock<br>Tell time<br>Lotto |
| 8. Linguistics Input | Ability to understand what is said through gestures and words | Gates Primary Reading Test, Type PPR, Form I | Action Rhythms record<br>Out-of-doors record<br>Oral commands<br>Written commands |
| 9. Memory<br>a. Immediate Rote | Memory for digits or arbitrary, unrelated series of items, to be recalled immediately, using both visual and auditory presentations | Visual: Monroe Reading Aptitude Visual Test III | Visual: Flash cards—<br>pictures, letters, words, phrases<br>Auditory: Naming letters, numbers, and words |
| b. Immediate Meaningful | Recall of rote details, content and meaning immediately after presentation | Monroe Language Test III—Visual Monroe Read. Apt. Auditory Test III<br>Durrell Listing Comp. | Nursery rhymes<br>Sentences<br>Poems<br>Paragraphs<br>Stories and events |
| c. Delayed Rote | Recall of items after time lapse | Detroit Reading Readiness | Same as for immediate rote but with a time lapse |

table 18 (*Continued*)

| FUNCTION | DEFINITION | ASSESSMENT TECHNIQUES | TRAINING TECHNIQUES |
|---|---|---|---|
| 10. Integration a. Nonverbal | Ability to combine discrete stimuli into meaningful whole | Jigsaw Puzzle<br>Raven Progressive Matrices | Graded puzzles<br>Frostig worksheets<br>Visual discrimination worksheets<br>Visual Motor worksheets |
| b. Symbolic | Ability to abstract qualities or meanings from stimuli and to form constructs transferable from situation to situation, using materials that are tangible, abstract, and numerical | Tangible:<br>  Concept Section,<br>  IV Test of Psych. Ab.<br>  Visual Decoding<br>  Calif. Test of Ment. Maturity, 6 and 7<br>Abstract: Monroe Language Test II, Lafayette Clinic Test of Numerical Concepts | Useful language worksheets<br>Verbal: Thinking Skills worksheets<br>Independent Activities worksheets<br>Supp:<br>  Who Gets It game<br>  Play Store game<br>  Play House game<br>  Lotto games<br>Numerical:<br>  Blocks & objects<br>  Number Readiness worksheets<br>  Arith. Readiness workbooks<br>Supp: Number Readiness games |
| 11. Linguistics Output | Ability to communicate and express ideas either through language or gestures | Verbal: ITPA–Vocal Encoding<br>Nonverbal: ITPA–Motor Encoding | Naming objects<br>See Ques. puzzle series 4 & 12<br>Picture books<br>Telling endings to stories<br>Telling simple to complex stories and events |
| 12. Integration Inferential Reasoning | Abstraction of meaning from oral material implied not explicit | Gates Reading Survey Grades 3–10, Form I (speed) | Reading Thinking Skills worksheets |
| Dominance | Establishment of preferred hand, foot, and eye | Harris Test | |

pared programs and materials for retraining, i.e., visual perception, visual-motor sequencing, linguistics, gross motor coordination. We felt it essential to consider in both evaluation and training the range of cognitive, perceptual, and motor abilities to evaluate relative strengths and weaknesses in each and to relate these to academic and behavioral maladjustment. More recently, other workers have also recommended the move toward comprehensive retraining programs.

# chapter six

# APPROACHES TO INTERVENTION

## An Approach to Intervention

Definition is not enough. We have said elsewhere that the CPM child benefits simply by having his group defined for him and then identifying him as a member, as long as this is done following a systematic procedure involving some objective measurement. The inevitable next step, however, must be the development of a program of intervention to improve the deficit functioning measured and to achieve thereby some improvement in academic skills and general adjustment. For people who have the responsibility for helping these children to make a more successful adjustment to school and to life, definition is not enough.

Even as this book has been in preparation, almost a full cycle of attitudes toward programs of intervention has been completed. It began with ignorance, was followed by some theory, which resulted in some "treatment," and concluded with some disillusionment and despair. Part of the difficulty may be that the aims of such programs have not been clearly delineated. Jensen (1969), for example, criticizes the programs for failing to raise the I.Q. of children participating. If the aim of such programs is to raise the I.Q., we would be the first to agree that intervention is probably doomed to failure. Our approach is based on the assumption that CPM skills, with which we are concerned, are on a developmental continuum and that it is possible through a carefully organized intervention program to bring a child through the various stages of development in relevant skills until he is at the point necessary to meet the challenge of academic learning. As we have stated, it appears that the I.Q. is an important piece of information about the child, but it will not necessarily, nor even probably, be altered by our intervention approach. Our research findings lead us to concur with Denhoff et al. (1968), who feel that "there is increasing evidence that functional behavior can be influenced—generally to allow the individual child better success in his school and his environment."

In the past few years some researchers have attempted to correct academic disability by training in specific skill-deficit areas. Although children with differing diagnoses were used in the various studies reported, the results from these investigations of special intervention with "learning disordered" children suggest benefits can be obtained. In most instances, the emphasis has been on one or more modality for retraining, such as visual perception (Lewis, 1968), coordination and orientation (Ames, 1969), reading and reading readiness (Roche, 1962). Only one study reports negative findings. Falick (1969), using perceptual-motor training incorporated into a kindergarten curriculum with a nonspecific sample, reports no significant differences between trained and non-trained groups in second grade reading performance.

More recently several authors have reported on the use of multisensory training, and although conclusive results of effectiveness remain sparse, these reports are encouraging. Silver, Hagin, and Hersh (1967) report the application of training in perceptual areas to two groups of boys with at least one year's retardation in reading. These people report encouraging initial findings; however, the final results are not yet available. Frostig (1966) reports the use of training programs in sensory motor, language, perceptual, and conceptual development, but while she anticipates that these training programs will have positive effects on developmental imbalances and on school adjustment and achievement, data are not available and for the time being we must trust Frostig's admittedly impressive subjective impressions as to their effectiveness. Bannatyne (1967) describes a number of possible remedial techniques to counteract specific deficit functioning, but again sufficient results are not reported to determine whether successes are a consequence of the technique or of possible factors, such as teacher personality or transference.

The more traditional approaches for correcting reading disability by utilizing remedial methods have not been favored with more definitive positive findings. Silberberg and Silberberg (1969, p. 211) observed from their review of the literature about children that "in other words, longitudinal studies of remedial reading demonstrate that there is increment often of a large magnitude at the completion of the remedial period. However, this improvement quickly 'washes out' and the children seem to sink to a level commensurate with their pre-remedial experience."

## Implications from CPM Retraining Study

Based on our findings from comprehensive diagnostic assessment that led to the conceptualization of the CPM child, a multisensory approach involving deficit stimulation was included and tested by means of a controlled research project. We applied our training methods to a group of behavior maladjusted public school children as described above. Our hypothesis was that children receiving specific training in CPM deficit areas would show greater gains than would similar children who received no training or received instruction in a traditional remedial classroom. We postulated that specific CPM training would facilitate growth in academic achievement and allow for more appropriate behavior at school and at home. The children in our study had previously been identified in the phase of the study described in chapter 3, so that we knew that we were working with the appropriate subjects for our kind of program which had previously been used experimentally in working with inpatient children at Lafayette Clinic.

Although research data is also meager here, some major conclusions from that experiment can be drawn and discussed. Our experiment demonstrated that with some specialized work offered in small groups, deficit functioning in CPM skills can be improved beyond what could be expected as a result of maturation and the usual school experiences. The first grade subjects in the training group showed the most improvement, implying that intervention of this type, preceding some of the regular class instruction with CPM training materials, has the greatest benefit when used at the earliest possible grade. These findings are similar to those of Heckerl and Webb (1969, p. 203) who concluded "that young children can profit from special instruction and that this instruction need not be delayed in the hope that developmental readiness alone will help the children learn to read." This conclusion is further emphasized by the findings that children who did not receive any form of specialized intervention showed no improvement in CPM skills and, in fact, showed some regress.

Since the large percentage of improvement in functional skills was demonstrated by the children in the first grade, the firmly held belief of many educators that early intervention yields most positive opportunity for change was substantiated. The possibility then of prescribing specific training procedures that take into consideration the academic levels achieved by the children would seem feasible. Such an approach would involve a comprehensive CPM training program followed by academic instruction for those children who have developed few, if any, academic skills, with minimal involvement in formal academic activities. This type of program could be appropriate for children at the first grade and below. Children in the second grade and above who have developed some academic skills but who have experienced failure could receive a combined program of CPM training and academic instruction. Close coordination of CPM training and academic materials would allow opportunity for the child to put his newfound abilities into immediate practice in the classroom and to see the positive results of his efforts.

The significance of early intervention at first grade level or below lies not alone in the services that would improve skill functioning but also has its impact by improving the child's capacity to cope effectively with demands made upon him, improving his self-worth, helping to avoid the emotional difficulties associated with repeated failure. From the standpoint of psychological health, early release of stress and help in developing competence will prevent the development of distortions in personality which we have described as likely to occur in the CPM child. We cannot support the idea with firm data, but we strongly suspect that one reason we achieve greater success with our youngest age group is because they have not had the negative experiences in school which lead to poor habits, inappropriate compensatory efforts, and patterns of avoidance. After four months in our program, 39 percent of grade one subjects were in the most improved category as compared with 32 percent of grade two, and 12.5 percent of grade three, or a gradual reduction in effects with the older children. Furthermore, grade one subjects who received CPM training in contrast to traditional remediation or no special intervention showed the greatest percentage of improvement in skills (56 percent). This points to the necessity for early identification of CPM dysfunction and the implementation of multisensory stimulation programs to precede introduction of academic instruction. A screening battery prior to the entry to kindergarten would be helpful in identifying such children and would allow for specific intervention before the child becomes involved in formal academic activities (Rubin, 1970).

## Alternative Models for Use of CPM Methods

Ideally, identification and intervention are employed so that learning disability and emotional problems can be prevented. Being realistic we recognize that many children are not identified until after they have failed or have begun to show disturbing behavioral effects, but we can recommend alternative methods. These may be listed as follows:

1. Children at the kindergarten level who begin to show patterns of avoidant behavior or demonstrate skill deficits may be further screened to determine the full range of skill weaknesses and strengths. These specialized programs of CPM training may be introduced before the kindergarten level. In these cases, formal learning instruction would be delayed until the child reached a criterion level of performance in the identified skill deficit areas (see Winterhaven, Florida, study).

2. Some youngsters at the kindergarten or first grade level may be identified as high risk because of their learning disability and/or behavior symptoms. With these children further understanding of their strengths and weaknesses can be provided the teacher by use of diagnostic testing batteries, allowing the

teacher to improve in her understanding and reducing the possibility of stress for the child. In addition, specialized materials can be provided so that the teacher can supplement the regular teaching experience. In these instances the use of non-professional teacher aides, who are experienced in our research, is highly recommended.

3. For children beyond the first grade level, depending on the severity of the behavioral disturbance or learning disability, the following may be applicable:

   a) For some children total removal from the regular classroom is required, especially those who are failing to benefit from regular classroom instruction or are under severe stress as a result of skill deficits. For them, specialized techniques are required if there is to be progress. These children are sometimes referred to as specific learning disabilities children for whom a specialized approach involving CPM training and remedial education is required.

   b) For some youngsters who demonstrate limited specific areas of weakness and whose learning disability is mild, consultation with the teacher about the nature of the child's strengths and weaknesses may be sufficient to help the teacher reduce stress in her classroom for this youngster and enable her to alter the demands of the curriculum sufficiently to maximize motivation and provide sufficient support for continued progress.

   c) For other youngsters, especially those who have delimited areas of weakness which severely inhibit academic progress, the provision of a CPM training specialist for supplementary training and remedial education for part of the day, apart from the regular classroom, may provide the most benefit. Thus, for some children with only a few deficits and with some academic skills, supplementary training and classroom adjustment may be sufficient to strengthen the child's performance. For some children the classroom teacher may be advised by the specialist consultant on the methods and materials applicable; for other children a daily session or two or three times weekly session with the specialist, apart from the regular class, may be the most beneficial.

The utilization of teacher aides in both the regular class and the special class has proved to be an effective means for increased individualization. Our experience with the aides in our project led us to view their selection, training, and supervision as worthy of much consideration if they are to be used effectively in the schools. The first consideration is the selection of individuals who enjoy working with children and who are able to appreciate a child's world while remaining at the adult level. Furthermore, in selecting individuals to work with groups of children who demonstrate maladaptive behavior, it becomes most important to choose those who have potential for accepting acting-out behavior in an objective manner, and who do not see it as a personal affront or a confirmation that the child is "bad." These kinds of attributes appear to be more important to consider in aide selection than does the educational level or experience with groups of children.

## Approaches to Relieve Stress at Home

In our project we were struck by the problems of family adjustment, the confusion in understanding the child's problem, and the disturbed attitudes toward the child because of his particular difficulties and failures. We have demonstrated that it is not always the presence of deficits alone that lead to severe maladjustment but that frequently it is an interaction to conditions in the family, attitudes of parents or other factors in the child, and the problems the child himself brings to the situation. It seems likely that if such extremely handicapped children are to be worked with in a school system, there has to be a concentrated effort involving the family. In some school systems there are adequate mental health personnel, such as school social workers and school psychologists, to play the necessary roles, both within the diagnostic assessment process and in devising and implementing a total treatment plan. Just as it is important for the schools to incorporate such mental health personnel in their system, recognizing the "psycho-educational" nature of the problem and its solution, so is it important for the child mental health institution to incorporate within its approach educational assessment and remedial methods combined with appropriate treatment personnel. We feel that, because our study did not involve such approaches with families, our results have been meager. Some children may require removal from the home for a period of time when they can receive the benefits of a total milieu in addition to CPM retraining and academic remediation. Other children, while remaining in an alternate school program, may require additional services from the school, such as speech correction, or from the mental health facility, such as psychotherapy or chemotherapy. The ultimate goals are identification of the high-risk pupil early, and intervention with programs and attitudes based on an understanding of the relationship of cognitive-perceptual motor dysfunction to learning disability and to maladjusted behavior.

Perhaps the principal impression to emerge from our project is that the child with learning problems and behavior difficulties is usually a multihandicapped child, but not necessarily in the usual meaning of handicap. He has CPM deficits but he is also likely to have personality problems, visual and other physical complications, and sometimes a family picture that both fails to offer support and may be overtly destructive. No one institution within the community can meet all of these problems; in working with the CPM child we can see clearly delineated the need for all institutions and practitioners to contribute their special resources to provide the needed assistance to these children—school, clinic, teachers, psychologists, social workers, and physicians.

# appendix A

*The 20-Test Battery Administration and Scoring*

## Introduction

One of the major products of this research is a battery of tests that allows for objective measurement of the cognitive, perceptual, and motor dimensions considered significant for adaptation at school. Although the Lafayette Clinic Test Battery is not to be considered as a fully standardized test, in this study it demonstrated its utility as a means of identifying and describing children with high cognitive-perceptual-motor dysfunction. In a later phase of the study, the expectation that the battery selected those children most seriously in need of specialized intervention was confirmed.

A 31-test battery, supplemented by other standardized tests, and an intelligence test (table 7) were used in comparing a sample of behaviorally maladjusted children with a sample of problem-free children, comparable in age, sex distribution, socio-economic background, and grade placement. The subjects ranged in age from six years and two months to twelve years and three months and were drawn in essentially equal groups from the regular first, second, third, and fifth grades. Subjects with tested I.Q.'s less than 81 were eliminated. There were thirty boys and twenty girls in each grade sample for both the experimental (maladjusted) and the control (problem-free) groups. The findings from this comparison indicated that the experimental groups on the average performed less well on the CPM tasks than the control groups, with the latter showing very little dysfunction. However, the experimental groups did not uniformly show poor performance. Sixty percent performed very similarly to the control group. Approximately 40 percent of the maladjusted subjects at each grade level, however, demonstrated a low level of performance which was matched by only three subjects of the control groups. A CPM dysfunction score (the number of tests on which the subject scored below the criterion score) was used to separate subjects into high and low dysfunction groups.

85

These clear-cut findings suggest the usefulness of this instrument in identifying which maladjusted children have significant CPM dysfunction, i.e., the ones who can be considered the most suitable candidates for special programming. A refined battery, consisting of twenty tests, was delineated, retaining the items with the highest correlations with the total dysfunction score (see table 10). Subsequently, using a multiple regression technique, a short form was arrived at retaining essentially the same effectiveness in identifying the high dysfunction subjects (see table 10). The refined 20-test battery is probably the most effective instrument because it contains representative items from each CPM area, providing information useful for educational planning.

It includes instructions for administration, test forms, and scoring procedures. These make up appendix A. Scoring examples are provided in appendix B. Normative data—both grade and age norms —are contained in appendix C. A Summary Score Sheet is included at the end of appendix A.

## Suggestions for Administration

The tests were devised to be objective measures, requiring a minimum of academic background of the examiner but depending heavily on training and experience in giving tests to disturbed children. The age norms available are limited because of the small sample size for each age group. Some investigators may wish to use the grade norms which are based on larger samples and also supply the criterion scores for more tests that discriminated significantly between experimental and control groups. The normative tables are supplemented by the full tables of means and standard deviations for all the tests (see appendix C).

Some of the tests utilized follow their source exactly (see chapter 3),others vary from the source either in administration or in scoring. The materials necessary for administration were also derived from standardized tests, such as the visual test cards of Test III-A (see Monroe Reading Aptitude). The materials for the visual perception tests (Tests I-E and I-F) involve the use of a paper tachistoscope whose source is the Durrell Analysis of Reading Difficulty (see bibliography).

## TEST I-B

*Visual Perception—Form Discrimination—Simple*

*Directions:* Read the directions as stated. Any mark such as a cross or circle is acceptable. All 25 items are administered.

SAY: Place your marker so that you can see just the first row of letters. Look at the first large letter, then find another which is
just like it on this side. (Show) Put a mark on it.

Assist pupils in marking the 0 to the right of the vertical line.
Explain that they are to mark a letter which is exactly like the first
letter.

SAY: Now move your marker down. Find the letter or word over
here (show column to right of double line) which is exactly like
the one in the first column. Put a mark on it. Now move your
paper down and do the rest in the same way. Now do all the
rest on the page.

Encourage pupils to do all the items on this page. When pupils
have completed the page or done all they are able to

SAY: Now turn to the next page. (Pause) Here are more words.
Find a word which is just like the first word. Put a mark on it.
Do all of these the same way.

In a group, the examiner may allow a pupil to turn to this last
page as he completes the first.

*TIMING:* Approximately 5 minutes.

*SCORING:* Each item is scored 1 or 0.

*MAXIMUM SCORE:* 25.

*Appendix A*

## TEST I–B

| O | M | O | R | S |
|---|---|---|---|---|
| 1. H | W | A | H | S |
| 2. F | P | F | E | D |
| 3. b | b | d | p | q |
| 4. at | to | of | it | at |
| 5. buy | any | cat | buy | for |
| 6. hit | get | sat | its | hit |
| 7. make | take | brake | make | mate |
| 8. clock | block | flock | click | clock |
| 9. protect | protest | promote | pretext | protect |
| 10. neither | neighbor | feather | neither | heather |
| 11. delight | daylight | delightful | detest | delight |
| 12. surprise | suppose | surprise | surpass | surplus |
| 13. property | prosperity | prophecy | probably | property |
| 14. vertical | versatile | virtual | vertical | verbal |
| 15. circular | circulate | cinerator | circular | circuit |
| 16. principal | principle | printable | primeval | principal |
| 17. modality | modesty | mollify | modality | modify |
| 18. coagulate | coaction | coordinate | coagulate | cooperate |
| 19. operation | opposition | operation | operator | opinion |
| 20. variation | vaccination | valuation | variation | vaporization |
| 21. continental | centennial | comptroller | contemplation | continental |
| 22. thermostat | thermoplastic | thermometer | thesaurus | thermostat |
| 23. liturgical | literal | liturgical | lethal | liberal |
| 24. perpendicular | perpetration | perpendicular | particular | perpetual |
| 25. heterogeneous | homogeneous | homologous | heterogeneous | histrionic |

RAW SCORE _____

From Lee Clark Reading Readiness Test by J. Murray Lee and Willis W. Clark. Copyright © 1960 by McGraw-Hill, Inc. Used by permission of the publisher, CTB/McGraw-Hill, Monterey, California.

88

## TEST I-E

*Visual Perception—Form Discrimination—Complex*

*Materials:* Paper Tachistoscope, Word List A, Marker.

*Directions:* Put in the tachistoscope, without the shutter, the card with Word List A. Expose Word List in the Record Booklet, and direct him to put a marker under the first row of letters. Show the first letter in the tachistoscope, the letter f and

SAY: See if you can find this letter in the first row. (If the child points to the right letter, tell him) All right, now draw a circle around it. (If he is confused and does not pick the right letter, tell him) Take another look at this letter (in the tachistoscope). Now see if you can find it. (Then have him draw a circle around it. After the first two items, warn him) From now on, you can have only one look. Be sure to look carefully when I show you the word. Do not move your marker until I take the word away.

Show the child the letter or word for about two or three seconds, long enough for him to get a good look at it. Usually the child will take a quick look. Then turn to the Record Booklet, move the tachistoscope card to the next word.

*TIMING:* No time limit.

*DISCONTINUE:* 4 consecutive failures.

*SCORING:* Each item is scored 1 or 0, including the example.

*MAXIMUM SCORE:* 20

*Appendix A*

# TEST I–E

1. y    b    d    g    *f* *
2. m    *h*    n    r    t
3. no   on   imp   *in*   nip
4. saw   war   as   *was*   waste
5. girl   *dog*   boy   dig   day
6. won   no   *now*   mow   was
7. lack   clock   *black*   block   dark
8. frost   *first*   fast   firm   trust
9. slat   *last*   lost   lot   blast
10. jump   jest   *just*   jot   must
11. clear   *clean*   close   climb   lean
12. par   park   trap   party   quart   dark   *part*
13. *quiet*   quick   quack   point   quite   question   quit
14. state   elation   tasted   *station*   *stationed*   started   skating
15. nomination   notion   mention   *mountain*   mountains   motion   mentioned
16. quarter   portion   bracelet   particle   *practice*   practical   poultice
17. obscure   advice   above   advise   advances   dance   *advance*
18. sure   obscure   scare   *secure*   second   server   cure
19. contact   contain   *contract*   contracts   contacts   capital   convince
20. immediate   meditates   mediate   mistake   *meditate*   material   meditative

RAW SCORE_____

* Words in italics are from Word List A.

*Appendix A*

## TEST I-F

*Visual Perception—Form Discrimination—Complex*

*Materials:* Paper tachistoscope, Word Lists B and C.

*Directions:* Subjects in Grades 1–3: Begin with the first letter of Word List B (1–20). Give the entire list until the child fails 3 words in a row. If he finishes Word List B, continue with Word List C (21–35). Failure is defined below as ½ credit or less per item.

Place in the tachistoscope the card with Word List B. Do not use the shutter. Show the child the first letter for two or three seconds.

SAY: Look at this letter (remove card after 2 or 3 seconds). Now write it beside no. 1 in the booklet in this column. (Indicate column)

Do not pronounce the letter or ask the child to read it. As soon as the child has looked at the letter, remove the card and have him write it from memory. Do not allow time to repeat the letter subvocally, but if the child does so make note of the fact. Show child the next 2 items in same way.

*Subjects above 3rd grade:* Begin with the first 5 items of Word List B. If subject makes any error, continue with Word List B as with the younger child. If the subject completes the first 5 without error, proceed to Word List C. If he misses full credit on any of the first 3 on this list, turn back to Word List B and continue until 3 consecutive failures.

SAY: Look at this word. (Remove card after 2 or 3 seconds) Now write it beside no. 1.

*TIMING:* No time limit.

*DISCONTINUE:* After 3 consecutive failures. A word is failed if the score obtained is equal to ½ or less of the total credit.

*SCORING:* Each correct letter in proper place is given 1 credit and the sum for each word is totaled. One-half credit is subtracted for each letter omitted, added, or out of place by 1 position, but do not penalize for incorrect portion of letters in the rest of the word. No credit is given or subtracted for an incorrect letter replacing a stimulus letter. Subtract ½ credit for letters added to the total word but do not subtract points for letters omitted at the end of the word. If the word can be scored two ways, give the larger score. Partial credit received for the last 3 consecutive failures is added to the total score.

*For subjects above 3rd grade:* If the first 5 items of Word List B are all correct and no errors on the first 3 items of Word List C, give full credit for Test B (99 points). If the subject makes any error on the first 3 of Word List C, and subsequently fails 3 items in a row on Word List B, then the items passed in Word List C are not included in the final score.

*Scoring examples:*

| Stimulus word | Response | Score |
|---|---|---|
| come | cone | 3 |
| name | naem | 2½ |
| chair | chai | 4 |
| canalize | canalized | 7½ |
| thorough | through | 6½ |
| thorough | thorght | 4½ |
| different | diffe | 5 |
| photograph | photografe | 8 |

1. d
2. p
3. no
4. saw
5. bag
6. wet
7. look
8. blow
9. lost
10. come
11. name
12. chair
13. sleep
14. afraid
15. chimney
16. morning
17. breakfast
18. different
19. photograph
20. thorough
21. welkin
22. ampersand
23. canalize
24. denotable
25. variform
26. wainscot
27. inception
28. monochord
29. tribunal
30. contingent
31. verbalist
32. brigantine
33. gangliate
34. quadruped
35. hydrostat

RAW SCORE _____

## TEST II-A

*Auditory Perception—Sound Discrimination*

*Materials:* Binet cards a* and b; tape recorder.

*Administration:* In order to eliminate visual cues and to reduce variations introduced by voice quality or accents of different examiners, it is desirable to present this test by means of a tape, prerecorded by a person with a clear, deep voice. Otherwise, the child should be placed so that he faces away from the examiner.

It is important that the subject understand the directions clearly. Young children in particular may not clearly comprehend what is meant by "same" or "different." The following introduction is used to explain these concepts.

Present card a.

SAY: See these two trees? They are the same, aren't they? Just the same. (Then show card b)

SAY: But these two aren't alike (pointing), one is round and one is square. They are different, aren't they?
  I am going to say two words. Sometimes the words will be the same; then you say "same." Sometimes parts of the words will be the same but other parts will be different. Then you say, "different." Let's try some words.

Practice items: (Examples)
"ma - pa" (Are these same or different? Different)
"boy - toy" (Are these same or different? Different)
"dog - dog" (Are these same or different? Same)
"tune - loon" (Are these same or different? Different)
"cat - cat" (Are these same or different? Same)

The practice items may be repeated, as needed, to be sure the subject understands.

SAY: Here are some more words. (Read items, pausing to allow a response. Repeat directions, "Are these the same or different" as needed. It is not permissible to repeat the word-pair once given.)

*Appendix A*

## Items

1. tin - thin
2. late - date
3. pig - big
4. (gun - gun)
5. test - text
6. bud - bug
7. chip - ship
8. habitat - habitant
9. sop - shop
10. conical - comical
11. (hoe - hoe)
12. beats - beads
13. cytology - psychology
14. class - clasp
15. mush - much

## Items

16. patriarch - matriarch
17. (peach - peach)
18. wear - where
19. biscuit - brisket
20. foal - stole
21. pass - path
22. convergent - conversant
23. falls - false
24. (at - at)
25. refracted - retracted
26. coke - cope
27. carrion - Marion
28. (far - far)
29. frisking - whisking
30. thigh - sigh

*TIMING:* No time limit

*SCORING:* Each item is cored 1 or 0. Record incorrect responses and no responses for qualitative analysis only.

*MAXIMUM SCORE:* 30.

| ITEMS | COR. | ERR. | NO RSP. |
|---|---|---|---|
| 1. tin - thin | | | |
| 2. late - date | | | |
| 3. pig - big | | | |
| 4. (gun - gun) | | | |
| 5. test - text | | | |
| 6. bud - bug | | | |
| 7. chip - ship | | | |
| 8. habitat - habitant | | | |
| 9. sop - shop | | | |
| 10. conical - comical | | | |
| 11. (hoe - hoe) | | | |
| 12. beats - beads | | | |
| 13. cytology - psychology | | | |
| 14. class - clasp | | | |
| 15. mush - much | | | |
| 16. patriarch - matriarch | | | |
| 17. (peach - peach) | | | |
| 18. wear - where | | | |
| 19. biscuit - brisket | | | |

20. foal - stole \_\_\_\_\_  \_\_\_\_\_  \_\_\_\_\_
21. pass - path \_\_\_\_\_  \_\_\_\_\_  \_\_\_\_\_
22. convergent - conversant \_\_\_\_\_  \_\_\_\_\_  \_\_\_\_\_
23. falls - false \_\_\_\_\_  \_\_\_\_\_  \_\_\_\_\_
24. (at - at) \_\_\_\_\_  \_\_\_\_\_  \_\_\_\_\_
25. refracted - retracted \_\_\_\_\_  \_\_\_\_\_  \_\_\_\_\_
26. coke - cope \_\_\_\_\_  \_\_\_\_\_  \_\_\_\_\_
27. carrion - Marion \_\_\_\_\_  \_\_\_\_\_  \_\_\_\_\_
28. (far - far) \_\_\_\_\_  \_\_\_\_\_  \_\_\_\_\_
29. frisking - whisking \_\_\_\_\_  \_\_\_\_\_  \_\_\_\_\_
30. thigh - sigh \_\_\_\_\_  \_\_\_\_\_  \_\_\_\_\_

TOTALS \_\_\_\_\_  \_\_\_\_\_  \_\_\_\_\_

RAW SCORE _____

* Reproduced from O. C. Irwin and P. J. Jensen, "A Test of Sound Discrimination for Use with Cerebral Palsied Children, in *Cerebral Palsy Review* 24 (1963) with permission of authors. Test cards from Test 5, Year 5, Pictorial Similarities and Differences II, *Stanford-Binet Intelligence Scale Form LM* (1960).

## TEST II-B

*Auditory Perception—Sound Discrimination—Complex*

*Materials:* Tape recorder, marker.

*Administration:* Read the directions as stated with the subject facing away from the examiner. Use of a prerecorded tape is desirable. Proceed at a rate that allows all the subjects to keep up. In group testing, examiner must circulate to insure that each subject is on the correct item. Emphasize clearly which sound is sought for each section.

### BEGINNING LETTER

SAY: Look at the row of things at the top of the page. Put your marker under the first row of things. Put your finger on the one in the box. We are going to find something over here (demonstrate those pictures to the right of the box) which starts with the same sound as the thing in the box.

  A.  Look at the leaf in the box. Now look along the row. What *starts* with the same sound as leaf? Is it drum, horse, lamp, or cat? (Encourage a verbal response.)

        Yes, *lamp* starts with the same sound as leaf, so put a mark on the *lamp*. (Check to see that child has marked the correct picture.) I'll say the name of the thing in the box, then name the other things along the row. You are to put a mark on the thing in each row that *starts* with the same sound as the thing in the box.

  1.  Move your marker to the next row of pictures. Look at the rabbit in the box. Now look along the row. What starts with the same sound as rabbit? Is it fish, hammer, chimney, or rake? Put a mark on it.

  2.  Move your marker to the next row. Look at the table in the box. Now look along the row. What starts with the same sound as table? Is it bed, turtle, nail, or pipe?

  3.  Move your marker to the next row of pictures. Look at the goat in the box. Now look along the row. What starts with the same sound as goat? Is it basket, fountain, cane, or gate?

  4.  Move your marker to the next row. Look at the key in the box. Now look along the row. What starts with the same sound as key? Is it pumpkin, faucet, kite, or mirror?

### FINAL SOUND

SAY: Turn the page. Look at the row of things at the top of the page. Put your marker under the first row of things. Put your finger on the one in the box. We are going to find something along the row which *ends* with the same sound as the thing in the box.

B. Look at the cat in the box. Now look along the row. What *ends* with the same sound as cat? Is it table, pipe, key, or hat? (Encourage a verbal response.)

   Yes, hat ends with the same sound as cat, so put a mark on the hat. (Check to see that child has marked the correct picture.)

5. Move your marker to the next row of pictures. Look at the dog in the box. Now look along the row. What ends with the same sound as dog? Is it saw, pig, rake, or turtle? Put a mark on it.

6. Now move your marker to the next row. Look at the lamp in the box. Now look along the row. What ends with the same sound as lamp? Is it sheep, leaf, barn, or faucet? Put a mark on it.

7. Move your marker to the next row. Look at the hammer in the box. Now look along the row. What ends with the same sound as hammer? Is it cheese, rabbit, flower, or apple? Put a mark on it.

8. Move your marker to the next row. Look at the book in the box. Now look along the row. What ends with the same sound as book? Is it ball, drum, cane, or sink?

## INITIAL BLEND

SAY: Turn the page. Look at the row of things at the top of the page. Put your marker under the first row of things. Put your finger on the one in the box. We are going to find something along the row which *begins* with the same sound as the thing in the box.

C. Look at the star in the box. Now look along the row. What begins with the same sound as star? Is it pumpkin, rabbit, stamp, or fountain? (Encourage a verbal response.)

   Yes, stamp begins with the same sound as star, so put a mark on the stamp. (Check to see that child has marked the correct picture.)

9. Now move your marker to the next row of pictures. Look at the chimney in the box. Now look along the row. What begins with the same sound as chimney? Is it hat, hammer, money, or church? Put a mark on it.

10. Move your marker to the next row of pictures. Look at the tree in the box. Now look along the row. What begins with the same sound as tree? Is it box, duck, nail, or truck? Put a mark on it.

11.   Move your marker to the next row of pictures. Look at the sled in the box. Look along the row. What begins with the same sound as sled? Is it bottle, door, slide, or leaf? Put a mark on it.

12.   Move your marker to the next row. Look at the flag in the box. Now look along the row. What begins with the same sound as flag? Is it barn, flower, hat, or fish? Put a mark on it.

## *RHYMING*

SAY: Turn the page. Look at the row of things at the top of the page. Put your marker under the first row of things. Put your finger on the one in the box. We are going to find something along the row that rhymes with (has the SAME ENDING SOUND as) the thing in the box.

D.   Look at the swing in the box. Now look along the row. What rhymes with (ends with the same sound as) swing? Is it sled, ring, box, or bottle? (Encourage a verbal response.)

Yes, ring rhymes with (has the same ending sound as) swing, so put a mark on it. (Check to see that the child has marked the correct picture.)

13.   Now move your marker to the next row of pictures. Look at the lamp in the box. Now look along the row. What rhymes with (ends with the same sound as) lamp? Is it faucet, moon, rabbit, or stamp? Put a mark on it.

14.   Move your marker to the next row. Look at the clock in the box. Now look along the row. What rhymes with (ends with the same sound as) clock? Is it sheep, sock, hammer, or leaf? Put a mark on it.

15.   Move your marker to the next row. Look at the fish in the box. Now look along the row. What rhymes with (ends with the same sound as) fish? Is it dish, pumpkin, chimney, or house? Put a mark on it.

16.   Move your marker to the next row. Look at the vest in the box. Now look along the row. What rhymes with (ends with the same sound as) vest? Is it box, drum, chest, or cat? Put a mark on it.

## *FINAL BLEND*

SAY: Turn the page. Look at the row of things at the top of the page. Put your marker under the first row of things. Put your finger on the one in the box. We are going to find something along the row that has the SAME ENDING SOUND as the thing in the box.

E.   Look at the church in the box. Now look along the row. What ends with the same sound as church? Is it sink, drum, cat, or bench? (Encourage a verbal response.)

    Yes, bench has the same ending sound as church, so put a mark on it. (Check to see that child has marked the correct picture.)

17.   Move your marker to the next row. Look at the cabbage in the box. Now look along the row. What ends with the same sound as cabbage? Is it leaf, box, pipe, or hinge? Put a mark on it.

18.   Move your marker to the next row. Look at the comb in the box. Now look along the row. What ends with the same sound as comb? Is it thumb, faucet, gate, or sled? Put a mark on it.

19.   Move your marker to the next row. Look at the crutch in the box. Now look along the row. What ends with the same sound as crutch? Is it pig, mirror, rake, or porch? Put a mark on it.

20.   Move your marker to the next row. Look at the fist in the box. Now look along the row. What ends with the same sound as fist? Is it chimney, chest, box, or hat? Put a mark on it.

## LONG VOWEL

SAY: Turn the page. Look at the row of things at the top of the page. Put your marker under the first row of things. Put your finger on the one in the box. We are going to find something along the row that has the SAME MIDDLE SOUND as the thing in the box.

F.   Look at the wheel in the box. Now look along the row. What has the *same middle sound* as wheel? Is it lamp, pig, leaf, or moon? (Encourage a verbal response.)

    Yes, leaf has the same middle sound as wheel, so put a mark on it. (Check to see that child has marked the correct picture.)

21.   Move your marker to the next row. Look at the knife in the box. Now look along the row. What has the same middle sound as knife? Is it rabbit, pipe, barn, or turtle? Put a mark on it.

22.   Move your marker to the next row. Look at the cake in the box. Now look along the row. What has the same middle sound as cake? Is it pitcher, drum, ring, or gate? Put a mark on it.

23. Move your marker to the next row. Look at the nose in the box. Now look along the row. What has the same middle sound as nose? Is it slide, comb, bed, or whistle? Put a mark on it.
24. Move your marker to the next row. Look at the cube in the box. Now look along the row. What has the same middle sound as cube? Is it truck, flute, ship, or cheese?

*MIDDLE SHORT VOWEL*

SAY: Turn the page. Look at the row of things at the top of the page. Put your marker under the first row of things. Put your finger on the one in the box. We are going to find something along the row that has the SAME MIDDLE SOUND as the thing in the box.

G. Look at the hat in the box. Now look along the row. What has the *same middle sound* as hat? Is it drum, lamp, bottle, or horse? (Encourage verbal response.)

Yes, lamp has the same middle sound as hat, so put a mark on it. (Check to see that child has marked the correct picture.)

25. Move your marker to the next row. Look at the sled in the box. Now look along the row. What has the same middle sound as sled? Is it vest, plane, fountain, or moon? Put a mark on it.
26. Move your marker to the next row. Look at the fish in the box. Now look along the row. What has the same middle sound as fish? Is it tree, nail, pig, or barn? Put a mark on it.
27. Move your marker to the next row. Look at the sock in the box. Now look along the row. What has the same middle sound as sock? Is it plane, key, pipe, or bottle? Put a mark on it.
28. Move your marker to the next row. Look at the duck in the box. Now look along the row. What has the same middle sound as duck? Is it cane, gun, chimney, or candle? Put a mark on it.

*TIMING:* No time limit.

*SCORING:* Each item is scored 1 or 0.

*MAXIMUM SCORE:* 28.

RAW SCORE_____

# TEST II-B *(cont.)*

# TEST II-B (cont.)

RAW SCORE_____

103

# TEST II-B *(cont.)*

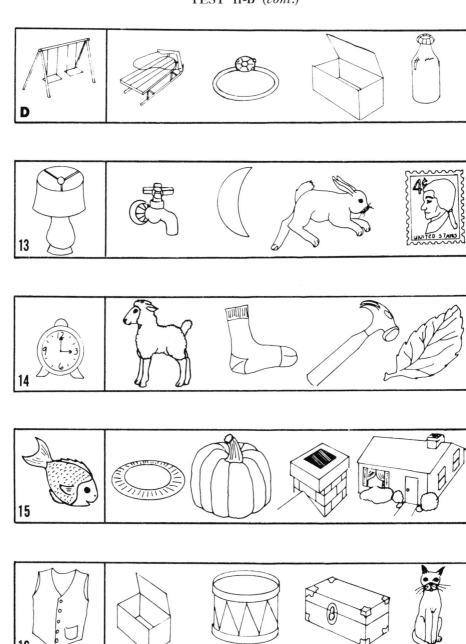

RAW SCORE_____

104

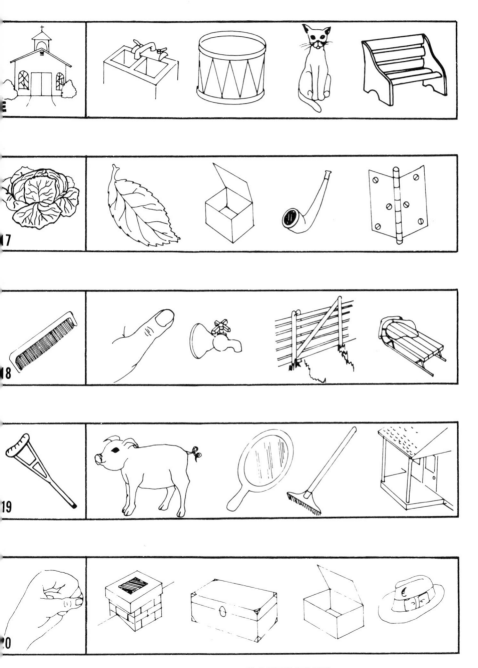

RAW SCORE_____

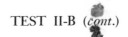

**F**

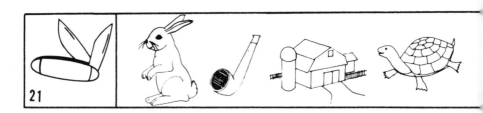

**21**

**22**

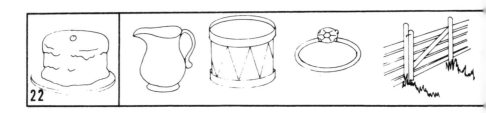

**23**

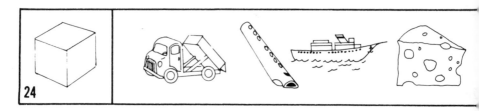

**24**

RAW SCORE_____

# TEST II-B (cont.)

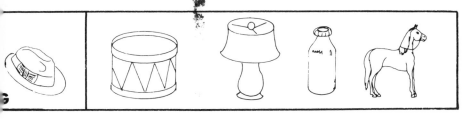

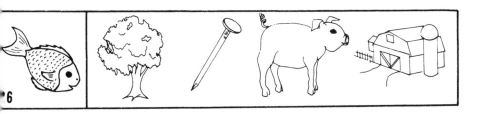

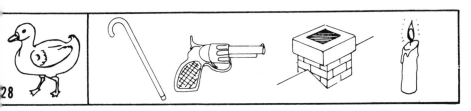

RAW SCORE_____

## TEST III-A

*Visual Memory-Form*

*Materials:* Visual Test Cards.

*Administration:*

SAY: We are going to draw some designs. I will show you some cards with designs on them. Look carefully at each card but do not draw anything because I am going to take the card away and *then* you can draw what you saw. Here is the first card. (Expose the first card for exactly 10 seconds and remove.)

SAY: Now, draw what you saw on line 1.

Proceed in the same manner with the remaining cards. Be sure to indicate the number of the card to be presented and the number of the line on which to draw.

*TIMING:* No time limit.

*SCORING:* A score of 1 is given for each correct element on a card. One-half credit is removed for each error, e.g., rotation, incorrect order, omission of part of figure. Two or more errors per element scores no credit. Credit is not removed for poor motor performance.

See appendix B for scoring examples.

*MAXIMUM SCORE:* 24

# TEST III-A

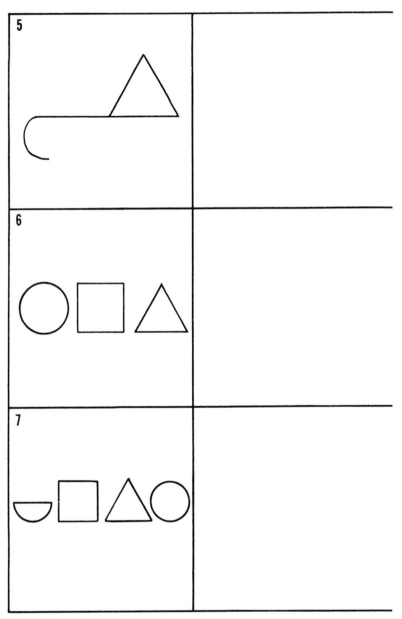

| | |
|---|---|
| **8** | |
| **9** | |
| **10** | |

SCORE:_____

## TEST III-E

### *Memory-Delayed Meaningful*

*Directions:* Read the directions as stated. Child is not presented with answer pictures until after another test has been interpolated. Interpolate test III-A or other nonverbal test.

SAY: I am going to read a little story. I want you to listen because I am going to ask you some questions about it after a while.

READ (with expression):

#### *Saturday at the Park*

Once there was a little girl named Jean and a little boy called Bobbie. One Saturday their father said he would take them to the park. They went on the bus. Jean wanted to put the money in the fare box and Bobbie wanted to put the money in, too. Father said, "No, Bobbie, you are too little. Let Jean do it." So father gave Jean the money and she dropped it into the box as soon as they got on the bus. On the way to the park they passed many things. On one corner they saw a little black and white dog. "When we come home, let's stop and buy him," said Bobbie. But Daddy just said, "We have one dog and that is enough."

When they got to the park, Bobbie and Jean both wanted to ring the bell to make the bus stop. Father said, "Your turn this time, Bobbie." So father lifted Bobbie up to the bell and Bobbie pulled the cord. The bus stopped and there they were at the park. Right at the gate to the park there was a man with a peanut stand. The children could smell the peanuts roasting. "Oh, I am so hungry for some nice roasted peanuts," said father. So he got bags of peanuts for everyone.

This park was like a zoo. There were monkeys, elephants, bears, and other animals for children to see. The children went to every cage and watched the animals.

At last they came to the bears. There were white bears, brown bears, and one big black bear and a baby bear. Father said, "Hey, Big Boy! Catch this peanut! He threw the peanut to the bears. Then Jean and Bobbie threw some peanuts. Sometimes the bears would catch them and sometimes the peanuts would fall on the floor of the cage. If a peanut went in the water the bears would swim and get it. What a time they had at the park!

Finally they got home. Soon the children heard the doorbell. Uncle Bill had come to supper. Uncle Bill was a big, jolly man. He sat down and listened while Jean and Bobbie told him about the park. Bobbie played he was a monkey. He did funny things. Uncle Bill just laughed and laughed. How he did laugh! He kept on laughing 'til mother called them all to supper.

They had a very good supper that night. Mother had made huckleberry pie and they had it for dessert. Uncle Bill liked the pie the best of anything they had for supper. "You know I like pie," he said. "And I do like pie!" They had a fine time that Saturday. Didn't they!

Examiner: The questions for this test will be administered after interpolated test is given.

### INTERPOLATE TEST

SAY: Look at the pictures. Some of them are about the story I told you. Do you remember the story about Jean and Bobbie?

SAY: Look at the row of pictures at the top of the page. Put your marker under the first row of pictures. Now take your pencil.

1) Mark the thing the children went on when father took them to the park. (Pause) If you cannot remember, wait until I tell you what to do next. Move your marker to the next row of pictures.

2) Mark the one who put the fare in the box. (Pause) Move your marker under the next row of pictures.

3) Mark the thing Bobbie wanted his father to buy. (Pause) Move your marker under the next row.

4) Mark the one who rang the bell when they got off at the park. (Pause) Move your marker under the next row.

5) Mark the animals the children fed. (Pause) Now turn your book over and put your marker under the first row of pictures at the top of the page.

6) Mark what Uncle Bill did when Bobbie played he was a monkey. (Pause) Move your marker under the next row.

7) Mark what Uncle Bill liked best for supper. (Pause)

*TIMING:* No time limit.

*SCORING:* Each item is scored 1 or 0.

*MAXIMUM SCORE:* 7.

# TEST III-E

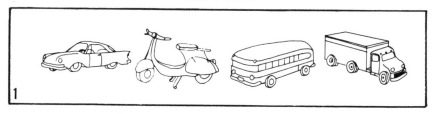

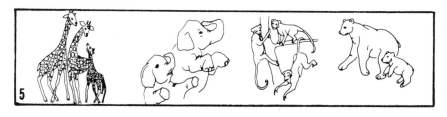

# TEST III-E (*cont.*)

RAW SCORE_____

## TEST IV-A

### *Orientation-Time*

*Directions:* The child is asked all 30 questions.

SAY: 1) How old are you now?__CURRENT WHOLE YEAR__
  2) When is your birthday?__EXACT__
  3) Have you ever seen me before?_____
  4) Have you ever seen me before you came to this place?_____
  5) How old am I?__WITHIN 10 YEARS__
  6) What day is it today?__EXACT__
  7) What day was it yesterday?__EXACT__
  8) What day will it be tomorrow?__EXACT__
  9) What is the name of this place?__NAME OF PLACE-IF SCHOOL-NAME OF SCHOOL__
  10) What kind of place is it?__SCHOOL-TYPE OF PLACE__
  11) What time do you eat *breakfast?* BEFORE 8:15 *Lunch?* 12–1 *Dinner?* 5–8
  12) What part of the day is it? (Morning, afternoon, or evening?__EXACT__
  13) What time is it?__ALLOW ANSWER WITHIN ONE HOUR__
  14) Where are you now?__NAME OF ROOM-LIBRARY, ETC.-OR-NAME OF SCHOOL-OR-PLACE__
  15) Is there another? (Name of place of testing)__USUALLY NO! "MAYBE" ACCEPTABLE__
  16) How long have you been going to school here?__TO NEAREST MONTH, YEAR.__
  17) Have you been in another?__(USE NAME OF PLACE)__
  18) Where do you live? (Address)__HOUSE # AND STREET__
  19) How long does it usually take for you get home from school?__(20–30 MIN. AS A MAXIMUM)__
  20) Where is your school? (Address)__STREET NAME OR CITY__
  21) How far from school do you live?__NUMBER OF BLOCKS OR REASONABLE DISTANCE (½ to ¾ MILE) —IF MORE THAN ¾ MILE ASK "DO YOU WALK?"- IF YES-MARK WRONG__

22) How long does it take for you to get to school from home?  ANSWER APPROXIMATELY SAME AS 19

23) Name the days of the week  (NOT HAVE TO BE IN ORDER)  ALL 7 REQUIRED

24) What day comes just before Friday?_____
Tuesday?__Wednesday?_____

25) What day comes just after Sunday?__Thursday?__
Wednesday?_____

26) Name the months of the year  (NOT HAVE TO BE IN ORDER) ALL 12 REQUIRED

27) What month comes just before September?__January?__
June?_____

28) What month comes just after November?__August?__
February?_____

29) In what month does summer begin?  JUNE

30) During which season do we have Halloween?  FALL, AUTUMN

*TIMING:* No time limit.

*SCORING:* Each item is scored 1 or 0. The examiner should adjust the answers to the item-16 and 17-to conform to local conditions.

*MAXIMUM SCORE:* 30.

Reproduced and adapted from M. Pollack and W. Goldfarb, "Patterns of Orientation in Children in Residential Treatment for Severe Behavior Disorders," in *AJOPs* 27 (1957), with permission of authors.

## TEST IV-B

### *Orientation-Size*

*Directions:* Read the directions as stated. Begin with item 1 and do not give any help.

SAY: 1) Put a mark on the tallest boy. (Pause)
2) Put a mark on the largest dog. (Pause)
3) Put a mark on the two little chickens. (Pause)

SAY: TURN PAGE.

4) Look at the tables at the top of the page. (Pause briefly) John uses the *smallest* table to draw on. Make a cross on the table that John uses. (Pause about 15 seconds for this item and each of the following items)

5) Look at the 4 dolls in the next row. (Pause) Jane's Daddy bought her the *largest* doll. Make a cross on Jane's doll.

6) Now look at the mittens Mother washed. (Pause) Make a cross on *baby's* pair of mittens.

7) Look at the baseball bats. (Pause) My brother plays ball with the *longest* bat. Make a cross on my brother's bat.

SAY: TURN PAGE

8) Now look at the pile of sand, the pile of bricks, the pile of rubber balls, and the pile of rocks. (Pause) Make a cross on the pile which is *lightest*. (Pause about 15 seconds after each item)

9) Look at the clothespin, the cookie, the spool, and the orange. (Pause) Make a cross on the one which is *heaviest*.

10) Look at the men walking across the ropes. (Pause) Make a cross on the man who is *heaviest*.

11) Look at the boys pulling the carts. (Pause) Which cart has the *lightest* package? Make a cross on it.

12) Look at the jars of paint. (Pause) Tony used the jar with the *most* paint in it. Make a cross on that jar. (Pause about 15 seconds after each item.)

13) Look at the boxes of crayons. (Pause) *Some* crayons fell out of the boxes. Make a cross on that box.

14) Look at the bookshelves. (Pause) Make a cross on the shelf that has only a *few* books on it.

15) Look at the wooden beads. (Pause) Mary wants to put them on strings. Make a cross on the pile of beads which will need the *longest* string.

16) Look at the scales. (Pause) Make a cross on the *lightest* bundle of wash. (Pause about 15 seconds after each item)

SAY: TURN PAGE.

17) Look at the bowl of fish. (Pause briefly) Make a cross on the *largest* fish in the bowl.

18) Look at the three shelves in the closet. (Pause) Make a cross on the boxes of food on the *lowest* shelf.

*TIMING:* No time limit.

*SCORING:* Each item is scored 1 or 0. Do not penalize for use of mark other than cross.

*MAXIMUM SCORE:* 18.

# TEST IV-B

# TEST IV-B (*cont.*)

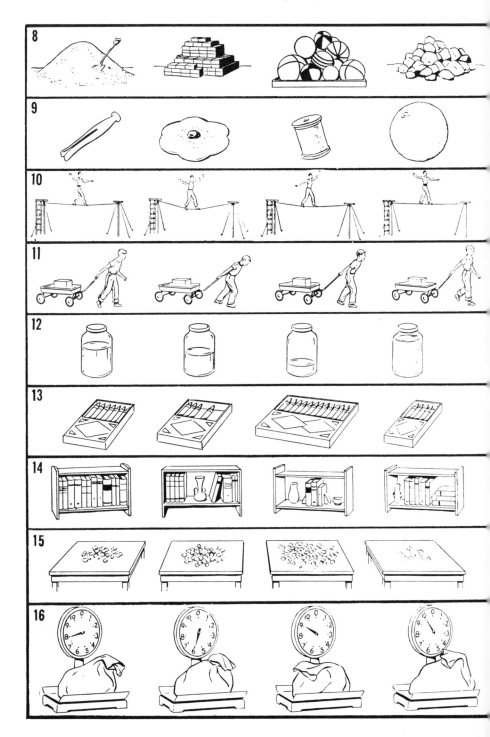

# TEST IV-B *(cont.)*

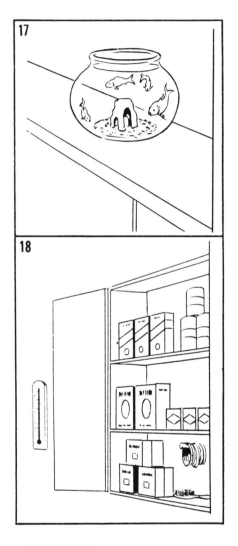

RAW SCORE_____

## TEST V-D

*Integration-Inferential Reasoning*

*Directions:* Read the directions as stated.

SAY: I will show you some pictures and tell you something about them. Listen carefully. When I finish reading, mark your booklet.

SAY: 1) Here are some toys for children. Draw a line under one toy that you think most girls would like best.

2) One of these three things can take you to camp. Draw a line under it.

3) Elsie learned that plants always grow toward the light. To test this, she put her geranium plant between two windows. She kept one window shade pulled down so no light could get in. Draw a line from the geranium to the window that it will lean toward.

4) Joe and Jean are going out to play in the snow. As they open the front door, Mother asks from the next room, "Are you children dressed warmly enough?" They answer, "Yes, Mother." Put a line under the kind of clothing they are wearing.

5) Until recently, all milk containers were made of metal or glass. They could be used many times, but washing and returning them was a bother to customers. Waxed cartons which can be thrown away, are less work. Put an X on the most convenient container.

SAY: TURN YOUR PAGE IN THE BOOKLET

6) Fred is going to build a model airplane. The wooden parts of the plane, a knife to shape them, and glue to hold them are all together on the table where they will be handy. As he begins to work, he finds something in his way. Put an X on it.

7) There are different kinds of horses for different jobs. The Percheron is a huge, strong horse that is used for heavy work. For riding, the fast sensitive Arabian horse is better. Draw a line from the rider to the horse he will probably ride.

8) Apples and pears grow on trees. Bananas, too, grow on tall tree-like plants. Most berries grow on low bushes, and some berries grow very close to the ground. Draw a line to separate the tree fruits from those that grow closer to the ground.

9) One of these boys will go to camp for the summer. Another boy will go to sea. Draw a line under the one who will go to camp for the summer.

10) Different coins are used in the different countries of the world. In Italy they use the lira, in Mexico they use the peso, in England they use the shilling, in Switzerland they use the franc, and in the United States they use the quarter. If you were traveling in New York City, what money would you use? Mark an X on it.

SAY: Now I will read some stories. Listen carefully. At the end of each story I will ask you a question and say some words which answer the question. You are to choose the word which best answers the question about the story. Let's try an example. Turn your page.

Read each story in a clear, interest-holding voice. Then read the answer choices, giving each equal emphasis. The answer choices may be repeated.

## PRACTICE ITEM

SAY: Let's do this one together.
SAY: The sun is hot. Boys and girls like to swim and play games on the grass. What time of year is it?
Winter   Spring   *Summer*   Fall
SAY: The correct answer is *SUMMER*.
SAY: Now we will do some others just like that one.
SAY: 11) They wiggled their pink noses and sniffed lettuce. Their long ears were flat against their heads as they slipped into the garden. What animals were these?
lions   tigers   dogs   *rabbits*
12) Mary was walking in the snow. She pulled her coat closer but the wind blew the icy snow against her face. What kind of day was it?
pleasant   warm   tiresome   *cold*
13) Mary was two blocks away when the school bell rang. She ran fast but all the children had gone inside before she reached the door. What was Mary?
early   *late*   sleepy   dead
14) The snow fell in great lazy flakes that soon covered the ground like a blanket. Tom got out his leggings and overshoes. It was very cold. It was now
spring   *winter*   summer   fall
15) On the table was a roast turkey with cranberry sauce.

There were also ears of yellow corn, pumpkin pies, and apple cider. For what was this table ready?

games    sale    wood    *dinner*

16) James brought out a rake, a hoe, a spade, and a sprinkling can. What do you think James was going to do with these tools?

*garden*    sing    shoot    fight

17) The sloth is an animal with hooks instead of feet. It can't really walk, but it can travel miles in the trees. What does the sloth like best?

plains    fire    mountains    *forests*

18) A frozen river between two mountains is called a glacier. It does not melt even in summer. How must the air around it feel?

mild    *cold*    hot    balmy

19) The blue roadster was in the ditch. The wrecking car got it out again with just one pull. What do you think the wrecking car had to be?

beautiful    *strong*    old    light

20) It is fun to have a clambake. Go down to the shore at low tide. Take a bucket and a shovel. What do you dig in to find the clams?

*sand*    plants    woods    buckets

*TIMING:* No time limit.

*SCORING:* Each item is scored 1 or 0.

*MAXIMUM SCORE:* 20.

# TEST V-D

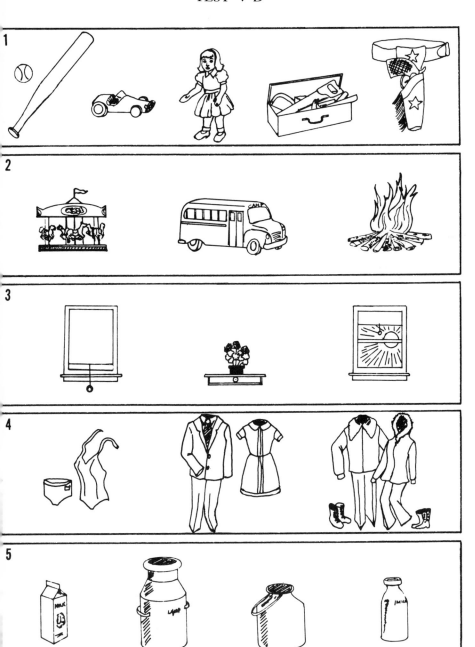

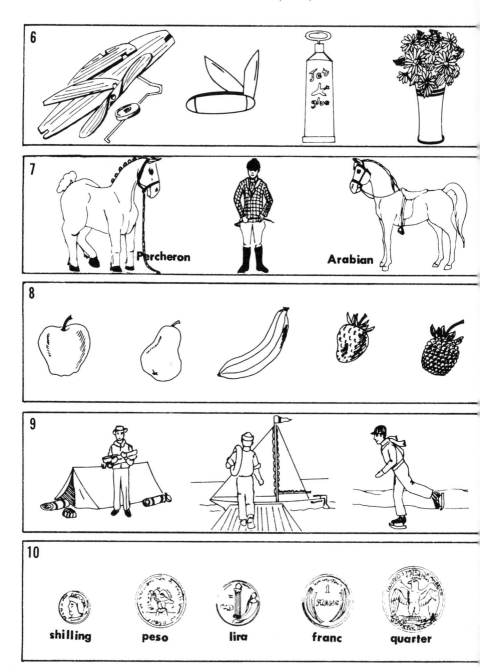

RAW SCORE_____

| *Sample:* | winter | spring | summer | fall |
|---|---|---|---|---|

* * * * * * * * * * *

| 11. | lions | tigers | dogs | rabbits |
|---|---|---|---|---|
| 12. | pleasant | warm | tiresome | cold |
| 13. | early | late | sleepy | dead |
| 14. | spring | winter | summer | fall |
| 15. | games | sale | wood | dinner |
| 16. | garden | sing | shoot | fight |
| 17. | plains | fire | mountains | forests |
| 18. | mild | cold | hot | balmy |
| 19. | beautiful | strong | old | light |
| 20. | sand | plants | woods | buckets |

SCORE_____

# TEST V-E

*Integration-Symbolic*
*(Numbers)*

*Directions:* Read the directions as stated. Subject may count with fingers if he wishes. Examiner may write down answers for items 11–15, if child needs help. Examiner may repeat the more difficult items once or more if needed.

SAY: 1) Count this row of dots. (Show line with 5 dots)
    2) How many dots do you see? (Show line with 10 dots)
    3) Now how many dots do you see? (Show line with 15 dots)
    4) Sue has six dolls. Cathy has five. Who has more dolls? (Sue)
    5) Jack bought 58 stamps. Alan bought 85 stamps. Who bought less stamps? (Jack)

Now show child Test V-E pictures in his booklet.
    6) Look at the glasses. Tom uses the second glass for his milk. Put a mark on the second glass.
    7) Look at the puppets. Sally made the fourth one. Put a mark on the fourth puppet.
    8) Look at the pieces of cake. One piece of cake is cut in half. Put a mark on that piece.
    9) Look at the six lollipops. We saved half of them for Diane. Put marks on the lollipops we saved for Diane.
    10) Look at the bricks of ice cream. Put a mark on the brick which is cut in fourths.

SAY: Write the correct answer on the line after I ask you some questions:
    11) Which is larger? ¼ or ½? (½)
    12) Which is smaller? ½ or ⅓? (⅓)
    13) Bob had $6.00. He spent ½ of his money for bike supplies. Bill spent ¼ of his $8.00 on models. Who had more left? (Bill)
    14) At a school candy sale, the boys each brought ½ lb. of fudge and the girls each brought ⅔ lb. of suckers. Who brought the most candy? (Girls)
    15) The Tigers have won 45% of all their games and the Twins have won 65% of theirs. Which team is ahead? (Twins)

*TIMING:* No time limit.

*DISCONTINUE:* On items 11–15, discontinue after 3 consecutive failures.

SCORING: Each item is scored 1 or 0.

*MAXIMUM SCORE:* 15.

*Appendix A*

## TEST V-E

1. ● ● ● ● ●                    Ans._____

2. ●●●●●●●●●●                Ans._____

3. ●●●●●●●●●●●●●●●●
   Ans._____

4. _____

5. _____

131

# TEST V-E (*cont.*)

## TEST V-E (*cont.*)

11. _____ —
12. _____ —
13. _____ —
14. _____ —
15. _____ —


NO. CORRECT _____

## TEST VI-A

### *Fine Motor Control*

*Directions:* The child is given a geometric form worksheet and is asked to identify each of the forms: "Tell me what you would call this," pointing to the circle, etc., down the page. If the child is unable to name, tell him as needed. He is told to reproduce each of the forms as accurately as he can three times in the spaces provided.

SAY: Copy each form. Do each one three times in the boxes. Do the best you can.

*TIMING:* No time limit.

*SCORING:* The geometric form worksheet is given five separate scores.
1) Circle and square are scored as a unit
2) Diamond
3) Composite form
4) Vertical lines
5) Horizontal lines

    The items are scored for accuracy of reproduction with emphasis on motor control. Poor line quality, erasures, marking over, all contribute to lowered scores. More than half of the forms for each scoring item must meet the scoring criteria to be considered for the higher of two possible scores. Scoring examples are provided in Appendix B.

    Each scoring unit is scored:
        1) Inadequate
        2) Transitional
        3) Adequate

*MAXIMUM SCORE:* 15.

*Appendix A*

## TEST VI-A

*SCORES:*

1. _____
2. _____
3. _____
4. _____
5. _____

### TOTAL SCORE _____

## TEST VI-B

*Eye-Hand Coordination*

*Materials:* Scissors, small envelope.
*Directions:* The child is given geometric form worksheet and scissors. Left-handed scissors should be available. Subject is told:

SAY: Cut out the forms as carefully as you can. Cut on the line. Put the circles in the envelope when you have finished.

*TIMING:* No time limit.

*SCORING:* The child's ability to cut on a line is specifically scored. The items are scored on *smoothness* and *accuracy*. Give one score for large and small circles separately. See Appendix B for scoring examples.
    1 = Inadequate
    2 = Transitional
    3 = Adequate

*MAXIMUM SCORE:* 4.

## TEST VI-B

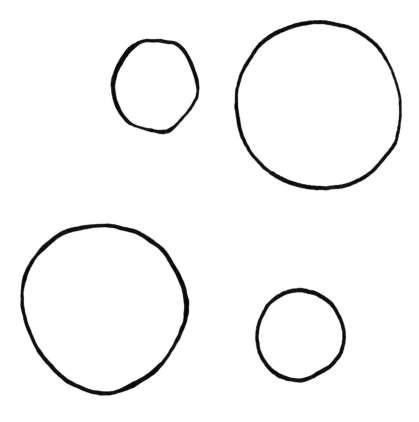

*SCORES:*

1. _____

2. _____

TOTAL SCORE_____

Reproduced with permission from Llorens and Rubin, *Developing Ego Functions in Disturbed Children*, copyright 1967, Wayne State University Press.

## TEST VII

### *Gross Motor Coordination*

*Directions:* The examiner should be sure the room for testing is adequately prepared in advance. Chairs, tables, or other objects, should be pushed to the side to make room.

SAY: Here are some things I want you to do.

*JUMPING:*
   A) *Both feet*
      Stand the child at the side of the room where he has a clear space measuring the length of the room in front of him. Ask him to put both feet together and to jump forward one step. The child must hold his feet together while he jumps and he must not step forward as in walking.
   B) *Right foot*
      Ask the child to stand on his right foot (show if needed) with his left foot off the floor. Now ask him to jump forward one step using his right foot only. During the task the left foot must not touch the floor.
   C) *Left foot*
      Ask the child to stand on his left foot and jump one step forward on his left foot only.
   D) *Skip*
      Ask the child to skip across the room using the feet alternately. Do not demonstrate.
   E) *HOP 1/1*
      Ask the child to stand with his feet together. Now ask him to hop on the right foot, lifting the left. Next, ask him to hop on the left, lifting the right. Now ask him to alternate hopping first on the right, then on the left. The child's body must remain in one spot during the hopping performance.
   F) *HOP 2/2*
      This task is the same as the foregoing, except the child hops twice on the right foot, twice on the left foot, etc.
   G) *HOP 2/1*
      Ask the child to hop twice on the right foot; once on the left; twice on the right, etc.
   H) *HOP 1/2*
      Ask the child to hop once on the right foot, twice on the left, etc.

*TIMING:* No time limit.

*SCORING:* These items are related to the child's ability to control his gross musculature and to alternate activities across the center of gravity of his body. There is also a factor of rhythm.

Each item is scored separately 1 or 0.

*Score 1* if the child performs task easily, no loss of balance, or stepping down with other foot when hopping.

*MAXIMUM SCORE:* 8.


## IDENTIFICATION OF BODY PARTS

Place the child facing the examiner at a distance of about 10 feet. Instruct the child to use one or both hands, as needed.

SAY: a)  Touch your shoulders
  b)  Touch your hips
  c)  Touch your head
  d)  Touch your ankles
  e)  Touch your ears
  f)  Touch your feet
  g)  Touch your eyes
  h)  Touch your elbows
  i)  Touch your mouth

*TIMING:* No time limit.

*SCORING:* Each item is scored separately 1 or 0. Score 1 if child performs adequately throughout, without hesitancy or confusion. He should point to both of the paired parts without "feeling around." Some allowance may be made for "elbows" item.

*MAXIMUM SCORE:* 9.

# TEST VII

*JUMPING (circle)*

| | | |
|---|---|---|
| A | 0 | 1 |
| B | 0 | 1 |
| C | 0 | 1 |
| D | 0 | 1 |
| E | 0 | 1 |
| F | 0 | 1 |
| G | 0 | 1 |
| H | 0 | 1 |

SCORE _____

*IDENTIFICATION (circle)*

| | | |
|---|---|---|
| a | 0 | 1 |
| b | 0 | 1 |
| c | 0 | 1 |
| d | 0 | 1 |
| e | 0 | 1 |
| f | 0 | 1 |
| g | 0 | 1 |
| h | 0 | 1 |
| i | 0 | 1 |

SCORE _____

## TEST VIII-A

*Linguistics-Input*

*Directions:* Read the directions as stated. This is a test of decoding oral directions.

SAY: I want to find out how well you can follow directions. I will tell you what to do with some of the pictures in the boxes. One repetition can be offered with sample items only.

*Samples*
    A)   Put an X on the ball.
    B)   Put an X on the milk bottle.
    C)   Draw a line under the little book.
    D)   Draw a line from the pig to the tree.

SAY: TURN PAGE
    1) Draw a line under the dog that is sleeping.
    2) Draw a line under the dark cloud in the sky.
    3) The father told the boy to put his pony in the barn. Draw a line from the pony to the barn.
    4) These boys are at their school picnic. They are running a race. Draw a line around the one who is leading in the race now.
    5) It is another rainy day. The children are going to school. They came in the school bus. They have umbrellas and rubber boots. Put an X on the place they are going.
    6) A child was told to hang his coat on the hook between the windows. Look for the place where his coat should hang, and put an X on it.
    7) This boy was very happy. He had saved a dollar to buy his mother a plant for her birthday. He found a store where they sold plants. Find the thing the boy had saved and mark it with an X.
    8) This little spider is spinning a web in the corner of the ceiling. The web is very fine and soft. Draw a line from the spider to the little window.

SAY: TURN PAGE

    9) At the Halloween party we had so much fun. We danced, played games, sang songs, and bobbed for apples in a tub. Draw a line from a child to a tub.

10) Yesterday the circus came to town. We saw animals and big wagons, and the clowns made us laugh. Make an X on the clown with black spots on his suit.

11) Two girls were caught in the rain. As there was no shelter, their teacher shared her umbrella with them. Draw a line from the smallest girl to what the teacher shared.

12) A cow produces milk, from which we get cream and make butter and cheese. From a steer we get beef. Calves' liver is a very important food for persons suffering from a certain vitamin deficiency. Put an X on the animal that gives us milk and cream.

13 The New York State Thruway is a superhighway. It crosses New York State. Another superhighway is the Pennsylvania Turnpike, which crosses Pennsylvania. Draw a line around the name of the highway that you would take to go from Albany to Buffalo.

14) Writing tools have changed since the United States came into being. John Hancock signed the Declaration of Independence with a pen made from a feather. Today people write with pencils, pens, or typewriters. Put an X on the kind of pen John Hancock used.

15) Here are three shapes: a circle, a triangle, and a square. The circle has no corners at all. The triangle has three corners, and the square has four corners. Draw a line from the shape that has three corners to the other shape that has corners.

*TIMING:* No time limit.

*SCORING:* Score each item 1 or 0. Directions for marking must be followed exactly.

*MAXIMUM SCORE:* 15.

# TEST VIII-A

Samples)

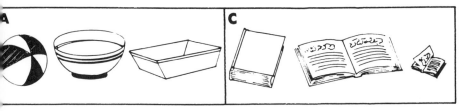

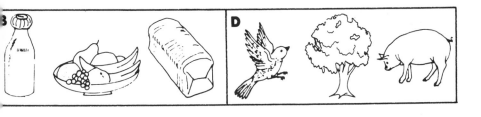

*BEGIN TEST:*

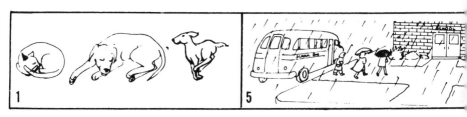

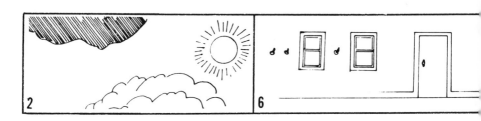

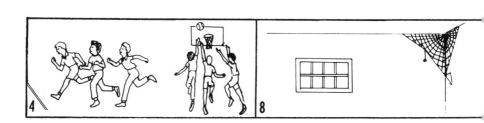

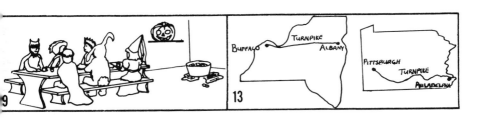

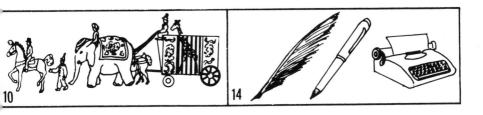

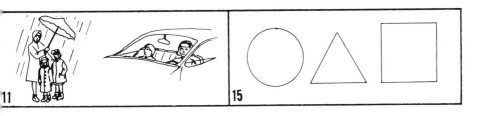

## TEST IX-E

### *Tactile Perception*

*Materials:* Blindfold.

*Administration:* Child is placed facing the examiner and is blind-folded. Examiner draws each figure on the palm of the child's dominant hand (hand you write with).

SAY: I am going to draw some figures on your hand. I want you to draw the same figure on my hand with your finger.

*Figures*

1) Circle

2) Plus sign

3) Box

4) Triangle

5) Short straight line

6) Angle point subject's left

7) Box

8) Half moon (opening to subject's left)

9) Angle point subject's right

*TIMING:* No time limit.

*SCORING:* Each response is scored 1 or 0. Responses to items 6, 8, and 9 may be in either direction, as recognition of form is being measured.

*MAXIMUM SCORE:* 9.

*Appendix A*

## TEST IX-E

1. Circle ○ _____

2. Plus sign ╋ _____

3. Box ▢ _____

4. Triangle △ _____

5. Short straight line ── _____

6. Angle point left ﹤ _____

7. Box ▢ _____

8. Half moon ( _____

9. Angle point right ﹥ _____

SCORE:_____

## *Lafayette Clinic CPM Battery Summary Score Sheet*

NAME_____GRADE_____AGE_____

----------------------------------------------------------------

### SERIES I
*Visual Perception*

B_____
E_____
F_____

### SERIES II
*Auditory Perception*

A_____
B_____

### SERIES III
*Memory*

A_____
E_____

### SERIES IV
*Orientation*

A_____
B_____

### SERIES V
*Integration*

D_____
E_____

### SERIES VI
*Fine Motor Control*

Total A___
Total B___

### SERIES VII
*Gross Motor Coordination*

4 Jumping_____
5 Ident._____

### SERIES VIII
*Linguistics-Input*

A_____

### SERIES IX
*Tactile and Kinesthetic*

E_____

BENDER KOPPITZ SCORE:___

RAVEN PERCENTILE:_____

FROSTIG

3_____
4_____

148

# appendix B

*Scoring Examples*

**TEST III-A**
**TEST VI-A**
**TEST VI-B**

## TEST III-A

*Visual Memory—Form*

Scoring Examples

| 1. | | |
|---|---|---|
| Score = 1 | Score = ½ | Score = 0 |
| 2. | | |
| Score = 1 | Score = ½ | Score = 0 |
| 3. | | |
| Score = 1 | Score = ½ | Score = 0 |
| 4. | | |
| Score = 1 | Score = ½ | Score = 0 |
| 5. | | |
| Score = 1 | Score = ½ | Score = 0 |

150

## Examples of Partial Credit

## TEST VI-A

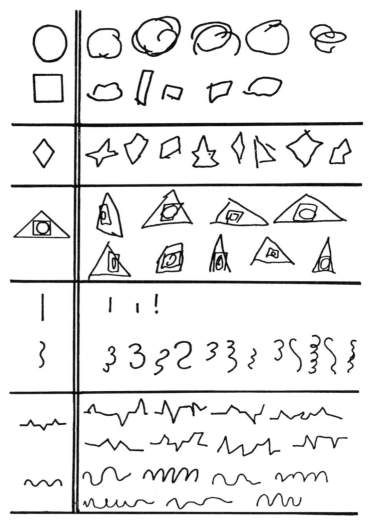

*Samples of Inadequate Performance on L-R Fine Motor Control Test—Score 1.*

## TEST VI-A (*cont.*)

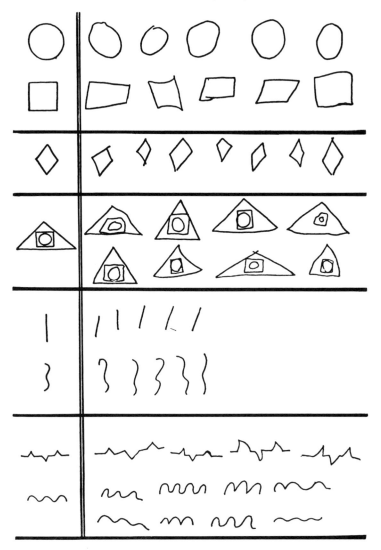

*Samples of Transitional Performance on L-R Fine Motor Control Test—Score 2*

# TEST IV-A (*cont.*)

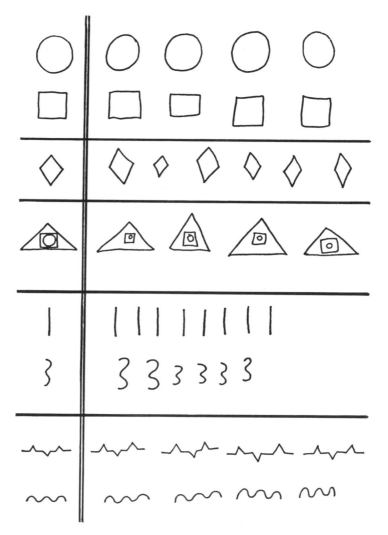

*Samples of Adequate Performance on L-R Fine Motor Control
Test—Score 3*

Reprinted with permission from Llorens and Rubin, *Developing Ego Functions in Disturbed Children*, copyright 1967, Wayne State University Press.

TEST VI-B

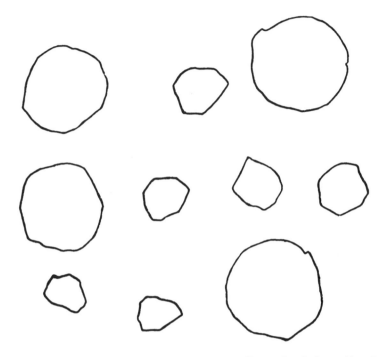

*Samples of Inadequate Performance on Eye-Hand Coordination*
*Test—Score 1*

## TEST IV-B *(cont.)*

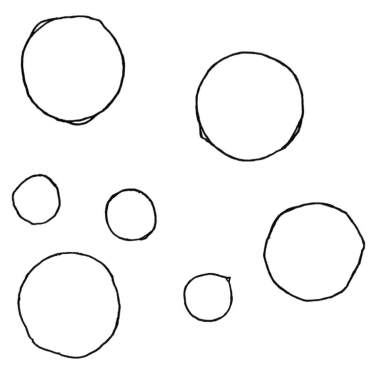

*Samples of Transitional Performance on Eye-Hand Coordination Test—Score 2*

## TEST IV-B (*cont.*)

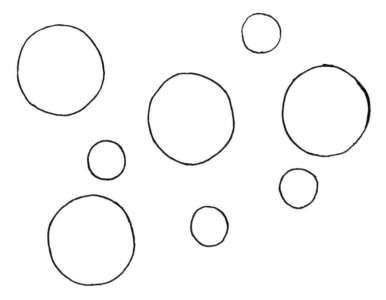

*Samples of Adequate Performance on Eye-Hand Coordination
Test—Score 3*

Reprinted with permission from Llorens and Rubin, *Developing Ego Functions in Disturbed Children,* copyright 1967, Wayne State University Press.

157

# appendix C

## Normative Data

### Grade Norms Data

In the original study, group comparisons between experimental and control groups were made according to grade. The means and standard deviations for each test by grade are reported in full in the research report. Those tests that significantly differentiated between the two groups and are part of the refined test are presented here. In addition, the cutoff score used to determine high CPM dysfunction is given in the last column.

### Age Norms Data

Age norms for children between the ages of six years two months and nine years seven months for each six month interval are provided for use when individual children are examined. In this way, a subject's performance may be compared on each test with the expected performance for his total age group. Thus used, a score that falls one standard deviation below the mean for the total group may be considered indicative of significant dysfunction. In addition, a subject's scores may be compared to the scores obtained by children from the original experimental group (behaviorally maladjusted) as well as those from the control group (problem-free).

### Special Instructions

In order to make sure of test score equivalence across age groups, when different forms were used, special scoring instructions were required. These are indicated on the age norms by Bender Standard. This score is obtained by using the Koppitz Scoring Method to determine the raw score:

$$\text{Bender Standard Score} = \frac{\textit{Raw Score-Age Group Mean}}{\text{Age Group S.D.}}.$$

## Cognitive-Perceptual-Motor Battery
### Grade Norms

| Test Name | Grade 1 6/2–8/4 | | | Grade 2 7/3–9/7 | | | Grade 3 8/1–10/11 | | | Grade 5 10/0–12/3 | | |
|---|---|---|---|---|---|---|---|---|---|---|---|---|
| | M | S | C | M | S | C | M | S | C | M | S | C |
| Frostig III | 9.2 | 2.7 | 7.9 | 8.7 | 2.1 | 7.9 | 8.1 | 1.6 | <7.9 | 7.8 | 1.2 | 6.99 |
| Frostig IV | 10.6 | 1.9 | 7.9 | 9.4 | 1.5 | 7.9 | 8.4 | 1.4 | <7.9 | 8.5 | 1.8 | 6.99 |
| Bender Standard | 6.9 | 3.7 | >12.0 | 4.5 | 2.8 | >8.0 | 4.5 | 2.9 | >7.0 | 2.5 | 2.5 | >5.0 |
| Raven Percentile | 17.8 | 4.2 | | 21.0 | 4.8 | | 21.5 | 4.4 | | 26.1 | 4.3 | |
| I-B-Vis. Disc. | 17.8 | 5.5 | 10.99 | 21.4 | 3.7 | 17.9 | 23.2 | 2.2 | 20.9 | 24.4 | 1.3 | 23.9 |
| I-E-Vis.Perc.-Const.-Raw sc. | 10.1 | 3.7 | 5.99 | 14.5 | 3.1 | 9.9 | 16.2 | 2.5 | 12.9 | 18.5 | 1.6 | 16.9 |
| I-F-Vis.Perc.-Const. | 35.1 | 22.7 | | 73.8 | 30.5 | | 105.8 | 42.5 | | 139.7 | 54.1 | |
| II-A-Sound Disc. | 19.9 | 5.1 | 13.99 | 21.9 | 4.2 | 16.9 | 22.5 | 4.3 | 15.9 | 24.7 | 3.9 | 20.9 |
| II-B-Aud. Perc. | 17.5 | 4.8 | 12.99 | 22.3 | 4.5 | 16.9 | 22.5 | 4.3 | 16.9 | 25.1 | 3.0 | 21.9 |
| III-A-Memory-Visual | 13.7 | 2.9 | 10.99 | 16.2 | 2.2 | 13.9 | 16.8 | 2.7 | | 18.0 | 2.6 | |
| III-E-Mem.Delayed | 6.3 | 1.0 | 4.99 | 6.2 | 1.2 | 4.9 | 6.3 | 1.1 | | 6.9 | 1.1 | |
| IV-A-Orientation-Time | 16.3 | 4.5 | 11.99 | 21.4 | 4.5 | 16.9 | 24.2 | 3.6 | 20.9 | 27.2 | 2.2 | 24.9 |
| IV-B-Orientation-Size | 15.4 | 1.8 | 12.99 | 16.5 | 1.3 | 14.9 | 16.9 | 1.3 | 15.9 | 17.4 | .8 | |
| V-D-Integ.-Inf.Rsng. | 13.6 | 2.9 | 10.99 | 16.0 | 2.4 | 12.9 | 16.9 | 2.2 | 13.9 | 18.3 | 1.7 | 16.9 |
| V-E-Integ.-Symb(Nos.) | 10.5 | 1.9 | 8.99 | 11.3 | 1.8 | 8.9 | 12.0 | 1.7 | 9.9 | 13.1 | 1.3 | |
| VI-A-Fine Motor Cont. | 9.2 | 1.8 | 7.99 | 9.3 | 1.6 | 7.9 | 9.8 | 1.4 | 7.9 | 11.6 | 2.0 | 9.9 |
| VI-B-Eye-Hand Coord. | 3.1 | 1.2 | | 3.4 | 1.1 | 2.9 | 3.3 | 1.2 | 2.9 | 4.3 | 1.1 | 2.9 |
| VII-Gross Mot.Co-Jumping | 5.3 | 1.9 | | 6.4 | 1.7 | 4.9 | 6.9 | 1.4 | | 7.3 | 1.3 | |
| VII-Gross Mot.Co-Identif. | 7.6 | 1.3 | | 7.9 | 1.6 | | 8.0 | 1.4 | | 8.4 | 1.4 | |
| VIII-A-Ling.Input-Total sc. | 12.6 | 2.2 | 9.99 | 13.4 | 1.6 | | 13.7 | 1.3 | 11.9 | 14.5 | .8 | |
| IX-E-Tact.Mov.Stim. Total sc. | 6.1 | 1.5 | 4.99 | 6.7 | 1.5 | | 6.9 | 1.5 | 4.9 | 7.5 | 1.4 | 6.9 |

M—Mean   S—Standard Deviation   C—Cutting Score

## Age Group—6 yrs./2 mos.—6 yrs./7 mos.

| Item | Experimental N = 25 Mean | S.D. | Control N = 13 Mean | S.D. | Total N = 38 Mean | S.D. |
|---|---|---|---|---|---|---|
| Frostig III | 8.0 | 2.2 | 10.8 | 2.4 | 9.0 | 2.6 |
| Frostig IV | 10.2 | 1.7 | 12.5 | 1.6 | 11.0 | 2.0 |
| Bender Standard | 56.6 | 30.5 | 75.4 | 22.9 | 63.0 | 29.5 |
| Raven Percentile | .5 | .9 | .1 | .8 | .3 | .9 |
| I-B-Vis.Disc. | 14.2 | 4.9 | 21.5 | 3.1 | 16.7 | 5.6 |
| I-E-Vis.Perc.-Const.-Raw sc. | 8.4 | 2.6 | 11.9 | 4.0 | 9.6 | 3.6 |
| I-F-Vis.Perc.-Const. | 21.1 | 14.2 | 43.0 | 8.7 | 28.6 | 16.4 |
| II-A-Sound Disc. | 18.3 | 4.7 | 22.0 | 4.7 | 19.6 | 5.0 |
| II-B-Aud.Perc. | 14.7 | 4.4 | 21.2 | 3.4 | 16.9 | 5.1 |
| III-A-Memory-Visual | 13.4 | 3.1 | 14.8 | 1.2 | 13.9 | 2.7 |
| III-E-Mem.Delayed | 5.7 | 1.4 | 6.6 | .6 | 6.0 | 1.2 |
| IV-A-Orientation-Time | 13.9 | 3.5 | 18.8 | 5.1 | 15.6 | 4.7 |
| IV-B-Orientation-Size | 14.2 | 2.2 | 15.5 | .7 | 14.6 | 2.0 |
| V-D-Integ.-Inf.Rsng | 11.8 | 2.9 | 15.1 | 2.5 | 12.9 | 3.2 |
| V-E-Integ.-Symb. (Nos.) | 9.6 | 2.0 | 10.6 | 1.4 | 10.0 | 1.9 |
| VI-A-Fine Mot.Cont. (Total) | 8.2 | 1.8 | 9.5 | .9 | 8.7 | 1.6 |
| VI-B-Eye-Hand Coord. (Total) | 2.7 | .8 | 2.8 | 1.2 | 2.7 | 1.0 |
| VII-Gr.Mot.Co.-Jumping | 5.0 | 1.8 | 4.8 | 1.7 | 4.9 | 1.8 |
| VII-Gr.Mot.Co.-Identif. | 7.3 | 1.3 | 7.8 | 1.1 | 7.4 | 1.3 |
| VIII-A-Ling.Input-Total sc. | 11.4 | 2.7 | 13.8 | .8 | 12.2 | 2.5 |
| IX-E-Tact.Mov.Stim.-Total sc. | 5.7 | 1.4 | 6.2 | 1.4 | 5.9 | 1.4 |

## Age Group—6 yrs./8 mos.—7 yrs./1 mo.

| Item | Experimental N = 19 Mean | S.D. | Control N = 23 Mean | S.D. | Total N = 42 Mean | S.D. |
|---|---|---|---|---|---|---|
| Frostig III | 8.1 | 2.1 | 10.5 | 2.1 | 9.4 | 2.4 |
| Frostig IV | 10.0 | 2.2 | 11.0 | 1.6 | 10.6 | 2.0 |
| Bender Standard | 47.1 | 24.2 | 68.5 | 25.8 | 58.8 | 27.3 |
| Raven Percentile | .5 | .8 | .2 | .9 | .1 | .9 |
| I-B-Vis.Disc. | 15.5 | 5.8 | 20.5 | 4.5 | 18.2 | 5.7 |
| I-E-Vis.Perc.-Const.-Raw sc. | 9.3 | 3.5 | 12.2 | 3.3 | 10.8 | 3.7 |
| I-F-Vis.Perc.-Const. | 33.8 | 24.8 | 43.3 | 15.7 | 39.0 | 20.9 |
| II-A-Sound Disc. | 19.0 | 5.8 | 20.6 | 4.9 | 19.9 | 5.4 |
| II-B-Aud.Perc. | 15.4 | 4.3 | 19.6 | 3.6 | 17.7 | 4.4 |
| III-A-Memory-Visual | 12.5 | 3.3 | 14.3 | 2.2 | 13.5 | 2.9 |
| III-E-Mem.Delayed | 6.4 | .9 | 6.7 | .6 | 6.6 | .8 |
| IV-A-Orientation-Time | 14.7 | 3.5 | 19.4 | 3.9 | 17.3 | 4.4 |
| IV-B-Orientation-Size | 15.5 | 1.6 | 16.2 | 1.3 | 15.9 | 1.5 |
| V-D-Integ.-Inf.-Rsng. | 13.2 | 3.1 | 14.8 | 2.1 | 14.1 | 2.7 |
| V-E-Integ.-Symb. (Nos.) | 10.0 | 2.5 | 11.4 | 1.6 | 10.8 | 2.2 |
| VI-A-Fine Mot. Cont. (Total) | 8.7 | 1.4 | 10.0 | 1.7 | 9.4 | 1.7 |
| VI-B-Eye-Hand Coord. (Total) | 2.7 | 1.0 | 3.5 | 1.4 | 3.1 | 1.3 |
| VII-Gr.Mot.Coord.-Jumping | 4.6 | 2.0 | 6.0 | 1.8 | 5.4 | 2.0 |
| VII-Gr.Mot.Coord.-Identif. | 7.3 | 1.1 | 8.3 | .9 | 7.8 | 1.1 |
| VIII-A-Ling.Input-Total sc. | 11.8 | 2.7 | 13.5 | .8 | 12.7 | 2.1 |
| IX-E-Tact.Mov.Stim.-Total sc. | 6.0 | 1.3 | 6.8 | 1.5 | 6.4 | 1.4 |

## Age Group—7 yrs./2 mos.—7 yrs./7 mos.

| Item | Experimental N = 18 Mean | S.D. | Control N = 27 Mean | S.D. | Total N = 45 Mean | S.D. |
|---|---|---|---|---|---|---|
| Frostig III | 7.1 | 2.4 | 10.2 | 2.4 | 9.0 | 2.8 |
| Frostig IV | 9.6 | 1.5 | 10.4 | 1.4 | 10.1 | 1.5 |
| Bender Standard | 55.3 | 28.3 | 70.6 | 22.3 | 64.4 | 26.0 |
| Raven Percentile | .6 | 1.0 | .3 | .8 | .1 | 1.0 |
| I-B - Vis. Disc. | 18.6 | 4.2 | 21.5 | 3.0 | 20.3 | 3.8 |
| I-E-Vis.Perc.-Const.-Raw sc. | 11.8 | 3.4 | 12.6 | 4.4 | 12.3 | 4.1 |
| I-F-Vis.Perc.-Const. | 47.7 | 21.5 | 63.7 | 39.1 | 57.3 | 34.1 |
| II-A - Sound Disc. | 19.9 | 5.2 | 23.0 | 4.4 | 21.8 | 5.0 |
| II-B - Aud. Perc. | 17.6 | 4.4 | 21.4 | 4.7 | 19.9 | 5.0 |
| III-A - Memory-Visual | 14.6 | 2.7 | 15.9 | 3.0 | 15.4 | 3.0 |
| III-E-Mem. Delayed | 6.0 | 1.1 | 6.4 | .8 | 6.2 | .9 |
| IV-A-Orientation - Time | 16.9 | 5.0 | 19.0 | 4.8 | 18.2 | 5.0 |
| IV-B-Orientation - Size | 15.4 | 1.2 | 16.1 | 1.6 | 15.8 | 1.5 |
| V-D-Integ.-Infer. Rsng. | 14.7 | 2.4 | 14.8 | 2.6 | 14.8 | 2.5 |
| V-E-Integ.-Symb. (Nos.) | 10.2 | 1.4 | 11.5 | 1.7 | 11.0 | 1.7 |
| VI-A-Fine Mot. Cont. (Total) | 8.9 | 1.5 | 9.9 | 1.8 | 9.5 | 1.8 |
| VI-B-Eye-Hand Coord. (Total) | 3.0 | .9 | 4.0 | 1.0 | 3.6 | 1.0 |
| VII-Gr.Mot.Coord.-Jumping | 5.3 | 2.2 | 6.7 | 1.5 | 6.2 | 1.9 |
| VII-Gr.Mot.Coord.-Identif. | 7.5 | 1.7 | 7.8 | 1.2 | 7.7 | 1.5 |
| VIII-A-Ling.Input-Total sc. | 12.7 | 1.5 | 13.0 | 1.7 | 12.9 | 1.7 |
| IX-E-Tact.Mov.Stim.-Total sc. | 6.2 | 1.5 | 6.3 | 1.6 | 6.2 | 1.5 |

## Age Group—7 yrs./8 mos.—8 yrs./1 mo.

| Item | Experimental N = 18 Mean | S.D. | Control N = 27 Mean | S.D. | Total N = 45 Mean | S.D. |
|---|---|---|---|---|---|---|
| Frostig III | 8.7 | 2.1 | 9.7 | 1.4 | 9.3 | 1.8 |
| Frostig IV | 8.6 | 1.4 | 9.9 | 1.3 | 9.4 | 1.5 |
| Bender Standard | 60.3 | 27.4 | 74.8 | 26.0 | 69.0 | 27.5 |
| Raven Percentile | .2 | .8 | .2 | .6 | .1 | .7 |
| I-B - Vis. Disc. | 19.6 | 5.6 | 20.0 | 1.8 | 21.6 | 4.2 |
| I-E-Vis.Perc.-Const.-Raw sc. | 13.6 | 3.5 | 15.9 | 2.6 | 15.0 | 3.2 |
| I-F-Vis.Perc.-Const. | 63.8 | 25.0 | 85.9 | 25.8 | 77.1 | 27.7 |
| II-A - Sound Disc. | 21.4 | 4.6 | 22.7 | 3.0 | 22.2 | 3.8 |
| II-B - Aud. Perc. | 20.2 | 5.5 | 24.7 | 3.3 | 22.9 | 4.8 |
| III-A - Memory-Visual | 15.4 | 2.4 | 17.0 | 2.1 | 16.3 | 2.4 |
| III-E-Mem. Delayed | 5.6 | 1.4 | 6.7 | .7 | 6.2 | 1.2 |
| IV-A-Orientation - Time | 20.2 | 3.8 | 24.1 | 3.8 | 22.6 | 4.3 |
| IV-B-Orientation - Size | 16.0 | 1.3 | 17.1 | 1.0 | 16.7 | 1.2 |
| V-D-Integ.-Infer.Rsng. | 15.2 | 3.1 | 17.3 | 1.7 | 16.5 | 2.6 |
| V-E-Integ.-Symb. (Nos.) | 10.5 | 2.0 | 12.1 | 1.5 | 11.5 | 1.9 |
| VI-A-Fine Mot. Cont. (Total) | 8.5 | 1.8 | 10.2 | 1.5 | 9.5 | 1.8 |
| VI-B-Eye-Hand Coord. (Total) | 3.0 | .9 | 3.7 | 1.3 | 3.4 | 1.2 |
| VII-Gr.Mot.Coord.-Jumping | 6.2 | 1.8 | 7.0 | 1.3 | 6.7 | 1.6 |
| VII-Gr.Mot.Coord.-Identif. | 8.2 | .8 | 7.8 | 2.1 | 8.0 | 1.7 |
| VIII-A-Ling.Input-Total sc. | 13.3 | 1.6 | 14.1 | 1.0 | 13.8 | 1.3 |
| IX-E-Tact.Mov.Stim.-Total Sc | 6.4 | 1.8 | 7.3 | 1.3 | 7.0 | 1.6 |

## Age Group—8 yrs./2 mos.—8 yrs./7 mos.

| Item | Experimental N = 23 Mean | S.D. | Control N = 27 Mean | S.D. | Total N = 50 Mean | S.D. |
|---|---|---|---|---|---|---|
| Frostig III | 7.7 | 1.9 | 8.6 | 1.3 | 8.2 | 1.6 |
| Frostig IV | 8.6 | 1.2 | 8.8 | 1.0 | 8.7 | 1.1 |
| Bender Standard | 53.0 | 28.8 | 63.7 | 30.5 | 58.8 | 30.2 |
| Raven Percentile | .6 | .9 | .0 | .6 | .3 | .8 |
| I-B - Vis. Disc. | 21.3 | 3.8 | 23.6 | 1.7 | 22.6 | 3.1 |
| I-E-Vis.Perc.-Const.-Raw sc. | 14.1 | 3.0 | 16.5 | 1.8 | 15.4 | 2.7 |
| I-F-Vis.Perc.-Const. | 73.8 | 31.4 | 109.2 | 34.0 | 92.9 | 37.3 |
| II-A - Sound Disc. | 20.7 | 4.4 | 22.2 | 3.6 | 21.6 | 4.1 |
| II-B - Aud. Perc. | 20.7 | 4.0 | 24.1 | 3.5 | 22.5 | 4.1 |
| III-A - Memory-Visual | 15.9 | 2.8 | 16.7 | 2.1 | 16.4 | 2.5 |
| III-E-Mem. Delayed | 6.0 | 1.6 | 6.4 | .8 | 6.2 | 1.2 |
| IV-A-Orientation - Time | 21.2 | 4.2 | 24.8 | 3.0 | 23.1 | 4.0 |
| IV-B-Orientation - Size | 16.1 | 1.6 | 17.4 | .6 | 16.8 | 1.4 |
| V-D-Integ.-Infer.Rsng. | 15.4 | 2.3 | 17.1 | 2.5 | 16.3 | 2.6 |
| V-E-Integ.-Symb. (Nos.) | 11.4 | 1.3 | 12.1 | 1.6 | 11.8 | 1.5 |
| VI-A-Fine Mot. Cont. (Total) | 9.0 | 1.2 | 10.5 | 1.3 | 9.8 | 1.5 |
| VI-B-Eye-Hand Coord. (Total) | 2.9 | 1.0 | 3.4 | 1.0 | 3.2 | 1.0 |
| VII-Gr.Mot.Coord.-Jumping | 6.5 | 1.7 | 6.7 | 1.4 | 6.6 | 1.5 |
| VII-Gr.Mot.Coord.-Identif. | 7.1 | 2.3 | 8.4 | 1.2 | 7.8 | 1.9 |
| VIII-A-Ling.Input-Total sc. | 13.3 | 1.8 | 13.9 | 1.2 | 13.6 | 1.5 |
| IX-E-Tact.Mov.Stim.-Total sc. | 6.5 | 1.6 | 7.1 | 1.1 | 6.8 | 1.4 |

## Age Group—8 yrs./8 mos.—9 yrs./1 mo.

| Item | Experimental N = 92 Mean | S.D. | Control N = 25 Mean | S.D. | Total N = 54 Mean | S.D. |
|---|---|---|---|---|---|---|
| Frostig III | 7.4 | 1.7 | 8.6 | 1.2 | 8.0 | 1.6 |
| Frostig IV | 8.0 | 1.4 | 9.0 | 1.1 | 8.4 | 1.4 |
| Bender Standard | 45.7 | 24.7 | 60.2 | 26.2 | 52.4 | 26.4 |
| Raven Percentile | 1.2 | 1.4 | 1.0 | 1.1 | 1.1 | 1.3 |
| I-B - Vis. Disc. | 21.7 | 3.1 | 23.8 | 1.5 | 22.7 | 2.7 |
| I-E-Vis.Perc.-Const.-Raw sc. | 15.2 | 2.8 | 17.6 | 1.5 | 16.3 | 2.6 |
| I-F-Vis.Perc.-Const. | 86.6 | 35.9 | 127.1 | 39.2 | 105.3 | 42.6 |
| II-A - Sound Disc. | 22.3 | 4.0 | 23.2 | 3.4 | 22.7 | 3.7 |
| II-B - Aud. Perc. | 22.1 | 3.7 | 24.8 | 2.7 | 23.4 | 3.5 |
| III-A - Memory-Visual | 15.7 | 2.7 | 17.4 | 2.3 | 16.5 | 2.7 |
| III-E-Mem. Delayed | 6.1 | 1.4 | 6.5 | .8 | 6.3 | 1.2 |
| IV-A-Orientation - Time | 23.3 | 3.7 | 25.2 | 3.4 | 24.2 | 3.7 |
| IV-B-Orientation - Size | 16.2 | 1.6 | 17.3 | .8 | 16.7 | 1.4 |
| V-D-Integ.-Infer.Rsng. | 16.2 | 2.3 | 17.9 | 1.4 | 17.0 | 2.1 |
| V-E-Integ.-Symb. (Nos.) | 11.6 | 1.6 | 12.6 | 1.6 | 12.0 | 1.7 |
| VI-A-Fine Mot. Cont. (Total) | 9.4 | 1.0 | 10.0 | 1.1 | 9.7 | 1.1 |
| VI-B-Eye-Hand Coord. (Total) | 2.9 | 1.1 | 3.8 | 1.0 | 3.3 | 1.2 |
| VII-Gr.Mot.Coord.-Jumping | 6.9 | 1.3 | 7.2 | 1.0 | 7.0 | 1.2 |
| VII-Gr.Mot.Coord.-Identif. | 7.9 | 1.6 | 8.6 | .5 | 8.2 | 1.3 |
| VIII-A-Ling.Input-Total sc. | 13.4 | 1.1 | 14.2 | .9 | 13.8 | 1.1 |
| IX-E-Tact.Mov.Stim.-Total sc. | 6.7 | 1.5 | 7.3 | 1.4 | 7.0 | 1.5 |

## Age Group—9 yrs./2 mos.—9 yrs./7 mos.

| Item | Experimental N = 12 Mean | S.D. | Control N = 8 Mean | S.D. | Total N = 20 Mean | S.D. |
|---|---|---|---|---|---|---|
| Frostig III | 7.6 | 1.5 | 7.9 | 2.2 | 7.7 | 1.8 |
| Frostig IV | 8.2 | 1.8 | 8.0 | 1.2 | 8.2 | 1.6 |
| Bender Standard | 31.7 | 22.3 | 47.5 | 30.0 | 38.0 | 26.8 |
| Raven Percentile | 2.4 | 1.9 | .4 | 1.0 | 1.6 | 1.9 |
| I-B - Vis. Disc. | 22.2 | 2.8 | 24.1 | .9 | 23.0 | 2.4 |
| I-E-Vis.Perc.-Const.-Raw sc. | 13.3 | 2.6 | 17.5 | 2.0 | 15.0 | 3.1 |
| I-F-Vis.Perc.-Const. | 64.1 | 26.4 | 149.6 | 50.3 | 98.3 | 56.4 |
| II-A - Sound Disc. | 19.9 | 6.0 | 25.4 | 3.1 | 22.1 | 5.7 |
| II-B - Aud. Perc. | 18.7 | 3.0 | 24.1 | 3.5 | 20.8 | 4.2 |
| III-A - Memory-Visual | 17.4 | 2.3 | 17.5 | 2.1 | 17.5 | 2.2 |
| III-E-Mem. Delayed | 6.4 | .8 | 6.4 | 1.1 | 6.4 | 1.0 |
| IV-A-Orientation - Time | 21.0 | 4.3 | 25.5 | 2.3 | 22.8 | 4.2 |
| IV-B-Orientation - Size | 17.1 | .6 | 17.1 | .8 | 17.1 | .7 |
| V-D-Integ.-Infer. Rsng. | 17.2 | 2.3 | 17.0 | 1.9 | 17.1 | 2.2 |
| V-E-Integ.-Symb. (Nos.) | 11.0 | 1.8 | 12.5 | 1.9 | 11.6 | 2.0 |
| VI-A-Fine Mot. Cont. (Total) | 8.3 | 1.5 | 10.4 | .7 | 9.2 | 1.6 |
| VI-B-Eye-Hand Coord. (Total) | 2.8 | .9 | 3.9 | .8 | 3.2 | 1.0 |
| VII-Gr.Mot.Coord.-Jumping | 5.9 | 1.6 | 7.1 | 1.3 | 6.4 | 1.6 |
| VII-Gr.Mot.Coord.-Identif. | 7.7 | .9 | 7.9 | 1.4 | 7.8 | 1.1 |
| VIII-A-Ling.Input-Total Sc. | 13.0 | 1.6 | 14.0 | 1.0 | 13.4 | 1.5 |
| IX-E-Tact.Mov.Stim.-Total sc. | 6.2 | 1.5 | 7.8 | 1.6 | 6.8 | 1.7 |

# bibliography

1. Ames, L. B. 1969. Children with perceptual problems may also lag developmentally. *Journal of Learning Disabilities* 2:205–8.

2. Ayres, A. J. 1963. The visual-motor function. *American Journal of Occupational Therapy* 17:130–38.

3. Ayres, A. J. 1963. The development of perceptual-motor abilities, a theoretical basis for treatment of dysfunction. *American Journal of Occupational Therapy* 17:221–5.

4. Bannatyne, A. D. 1967. Matching remedial methods with specific deficits. *Proceedings, International Convocation on Learning Disabilities.* Pittsburgh: Home for Crippled Children.

5. Barsch, R. H. 1962. Learning disorders of handicapped children. *Journal of Rehabilitation* 28, 5:10–12.

6. Bateman, B. 1964. Learning disabilities—an overview. Paper presented at Council of Exceptional Children annual meeting, Chicago, Illinois.

7. Clements, S. 1966. Minimal brain dysfunction in children. *NINDB Monograph no. 3.* United States Department of Health, Education and Welfare.

8. Cruickshank, W. et al. 1961. A *teaching method for brain-injured and hyperactive children.* Syracuse N.Y.: Syracuse University Press.

9. DeHirsch, K. 1963. Plasticity and language disabilities. Paper presented at the annual meeting of American Orthopsychiatric Association, Washington, D.C.

10. DeHirsch, K.; Jansky, J.; and Langford, W. 1966. *Predicting reading Failure.* New York: Harper and Row.

11. Delacato, C. H. 1959. *Treatment and prevention of reading problems, a neuropsychological approach*. Springfield, Ill.: Charles C. Thomas Co.

12. Denhoff, E. et al. 1968. Developmental and predictive characteristics of items from the Meeting Street school screening test. *Developmental Medicine and Child Neurology* 10:220–32.

13. Detroit Board of Education. 1962. Detroit Reading Readiness Test. 1st ed., 1945. School district, Detroit, Mich.

14. Doman, R. J. et al. 1960. Children with severe brain injuries, *JAMA* 174:257–62.

15. Dunn, L. M. 1965. Minimal brain dysfunction: a dilemma for educators. Unpublished paper. George Peabody College Institute on Mental Retardation and Intellectual Development.

16. Durrell, D. D. *Durrell Analysis of Reading Difficulty*. 1937, 1955. New York: Harcourt, Brace and World, Inc.

17. Eisenberg, L. 1957. Psychiatric implications of brain damage in children, *PQ* 31:72–92.

18. Falick, L. H. 1969. The effects of special perceptual-motor training in kindergarten on reading readiness and on second-grade reading performance. *Journal of Learning Disabilities* 2:395–402.

19. Frostig, M.; Lefever, D.; and Whittlesey, J. June 1961. A developmental test of visual perception for evaluating normal and neurologically handicapped children. *PMS* 12:383–94.

20. Frostig, M. 1968. Education for children with learning disabilities. In H. Myklebust, *Progress in learning disabilities*, vol. i. New York: Grune & Stratton.

21. Gates, A. I. 1942. Gates reading survey for grades 3 through 10. 1st ed. 1939. New York: Bureau of Publications, Teachers College, Columbia University.

22. Goldfarb, W. 1961. The mutual impact of mother and child in childhood schizophrenia. *AJOPs* 31:738–47.

23. Goldfarb, W. 1963. Self awareness in schizophrenic children. *Archives of General Psychiatry* 8, 1:47–60.

24. Heckerl, J. and Webb, S. 1969. An educational approach to the treatment of children with learning disabilities. *Journal of Learning Disabilities* 2:199–204.

25. Irwin, O. C. and Jensen, P. J. 1963. A test of sound discrimination for use with cerebral-palsied children. *Cerebral Palsy Review* 24:5–11.

26. Jensen, A. 1969. How much can we boost IQ and scholastic achievement? *Harvard Educational Review* 31(1):1–123.

27. Kephart, N. 1962. *The slow learner in the classroom.* Columbus, O.: Charles E. Merrill Books, Inc.

28. Koppitz, E. 1963. *The Bender-Gestalt test for young children.* New York: Grune & Stratton.

29. Lee, J. M., and Clark, W. W. 1960. Lee-Clark reading readiness test. New York: McGraw-Hill, Inc.

30. Leton, D. A. 1967. A new frontier in special education. In E. C. Frierson and W. B. Barbe, *Educating Children with Learning Disabilities.* New York: Appleton-Century-Crofts, p. 111.

31. Lewis, J. N. 1968. The improvement of reading ability through a developmental program in visual perception. *Journal of learning disabilities* 1:652–53.

32. Llorens, L., and Rubin, E. Z. 1967. *Developing ego functions in disturbed children—occupational therapy in milieu.* Detroit, Mich.: Wayne State University Press.

33. Maslow, P. 1965. Development, assessment and remediation of perceptual functions. Paper presented at annual meeting of American Psychological Association, Chicago, Ill.

34. Monroe, M. 1935. Monore reading aptitude test. Boston: Houghton, Mifflin Co., Cambridge: Riverside Press.

35. Mora, G. et al. 1968. Implications of neurological findings for residential education. *AJOPs* 38:643–46.

36. Pollack, M., and Goldfarb, W. 1957. Patterns of orientation in children in residential treatment for severe behavior disorders. *AJOPs* 27:538–52.

37. Raven, J. C. 1958. *Guide to using the coloured progressive matrices.* London: H. K. Lewis & Co.

38. Roche, H. 1962. Junior primary in the Van Dyke level plan. *JER* 40:232–33.

39. Rubin, E. Z.; Simon, C. B.; Betwee, M. C. 1966. *Emotionally handicapped children and the elementary school*. Detroit, Mich.: Wayne State University Press.

40. Rubin, E. Z. 1970. A psycho-educational model for school mental health planning. *Community Mental Health Journal* 6:31–39.

41. Silberberg, N. E., and Silberberg, M. C. 1969. Methods in remedial education. *Journal of Learning Disabilities*, 2:209–17.

42. Silver, A.; Hagin, R.; Hersh, M. 1967. "Reading disability: teaching through stimulation of deficit perceptual areas." *AJOPs* 37:744–52.

43. Strauss, A. A., and Lehtinen, L. E. 1947. *Psychopathology and education of the brain-injured child*. New York: Grune & Stratton.

44. Winterhaven Study of Perceptual Learning. A preliminary report. 1962. Winterhaven Lions Research Foundation, Inc., Florida.

45. Wrightstone, J. W. et al. 1956. New York test of arithmetical meanings. Yonkers-on-the-Hudson, N. Y.: World Book Co.

# INDEX

Eli Z. Rubin is director of the Northeast Guidance Center, Detroit, Michigan, and professor of psychology, Wayne State University. He received his B.A. (1943) from Harvard University, his M.A. (1947) and Ph.D. (1951) from Boston University.

Jean S. Braun is associate professor of psychology at Oakland University, Rochester, Michigan. She received her B.A. (1942) from the University of Michigan and her M.A. (1957) and Ph.D. (1961) from Wayne State University.

Gayle R. Beck is school psychologist, West Bloomfield Public Schools, West Bloomfield, Michigan. She received her B.A. in Special Education (1960) and her M.Ed. (1963) from Wayne State University.

Lela A. Llorens is associate professor of occupational therapy in the College of Allied Health Professions at the University of Florida. She received her B.S. (1953) from Western Michigan University and her M.A. (1962) from Wayne State University.

This manuscript was edited by Marguerite C. Wallace. The book was designed by Don Ross. The type face for the text is Linotype Janson originally cut by Nickolas Kis about 1690; and the display face is Perpetua designed by Eric Gill about 1929.

The text is printed on 60 lb. Sebago offset Antique paper; and the book is bound in Joanna Mills' Kennett cloth over binders' boards. Manufactured in the United States of America.